365 Easy Slow Cooker Recipes

Cookbook Resources LLC
Highland Village, Texas

365 Easy Slow Cooker Recipes
Simple, Delicious Soups & Stews to Warm the Heart

1st Printing - March 2008
2nd Printing - December 2008

International Standard Book Number: 978-1-59769-039-3

Library of Congress Number: 2008008980

Library of Congress Cataloging-in-Publication Data

    365 easy slow cooker recipes : simple, delicious soups & stews to warm the heart.
       p. cm.
   Includes index.
   ISBN 978-1-59769-039-3
   1. Electric cookery, Slow. 2. Quick and easy cookery. I. Cookbook Resources, LLC. II. Title:
Three hundred sixty-five easy slow cooker recipes.
   TX827.A1575 2008
   641.5'884--dc22

                        2008008980

Cover by Nancy Bohanan
Illustrations by Nancy Murphy Griffith

Edited, Designed and Published in the
United States of America by
Cookbook Resources, LLC
541 Doubletree Drive
Highland Village, Texas 75077

Toll free 866-229-2665

www.cookbookresources.com

cookbook **resources**® LLC
Bringing Family and Friends to the Table

Introduction

Born of necessity, these convenient slow cookers make life easier for anyone who uses them. Put your food inside, cover the pot, turn the switch to "on" and come home after hours of errands, soccer games, meetings, work or play and dinner is ready! Meals are simple, convenient and much better than any fast-food, drive-through-window meal.

365 Easy Slow Cooker Recipes provides recipes for beef, chicken, seafood, vegetables, soups and casseroles that are great as one-dish meals or as accompaniments to a main dish.

These recipes are family tested and used everyday by moms, dads, seniors, teens and college students. They are packed with nutritious ingredients, economical, wholesome and practical.

The recipes are easy, simple and everyday cooking that everybody loves. They are ones families grow up on and ones we remember long after adulthood. They are recipes that give you a warm and fuzzy feeling and let you know someone cares about you.

These recipes should never be taken for granted or passed by because they are too simple or too "normal". They are the recipes that strengthen our families and bring us the happiness and satisfaction of being together for a homecooked meal.

Contents

Introduction 3

Dedication 6

Appetizers. 7

Dips, Spreads, Wings & Smokies

Soup's On! 25

Soups, Stews, Chowders & Jambalayas

Veggies & Side Dishes. 97

Baked, Braised, Crunched & Stewed

Beef 133

Roasted, Smothered & Chopped

Contents

Chicken & Turkey 179

Honey-Baked, Oranged & Noodled

Pork & Seafood 247

Chops, Loins, Loaves & Hams

Desserts 293

Breaded, Fondued, Fruited & Fudged

Index 304

Cookbooks Published by Cookbook Resources 318

Dedication

With a mission of helping you bring family and friends to the table, Cookbook Resources strives to make family meals and entertaining friends simple, easy and delicious.

We recognize the importance of a meal together as a means of building family bonds with memories and traditions that will be treasured for a lifetime. It is an opportunity to sit down with each other and share more than food.

This cookbook is dedicated with gratitude and respect for all those who show their love with homecooked meals, bringing family and friends to the table.

More and more statistical studies are finding that family meals play a significant role in childhood development. Children who eat with their families four or more nights per week are healthier, make better grades, score higher on aptitude tests and are less likely to have problems with drugs.

Appetizers

Dips, Spreads, Wings & Smokies

Appetizers Contents

Unbelievable Crab Dip 9
Crab Dip 9
Broccoli Dip .10
Hot Southwest Dip 10
Cheesy Bacon Dip. 11
Hamburger Dip 12
Hot Broccoli Dip. 13
Indian-Corn Dip 13
Chicken-Enchilada Dip. 14
Pepperoni Dip. 15
Sausage-Hamburger Dip 16
Whiz Bang Dip 17

The Big Dipper 17
Firecrackers and Bacon. 18
Great Balls of Fire 19
Hot Reuben Spread 19
Crab-Artichoke Spread 20
Party Smokies. 20
Sausage-Pineapple Bits. 21
Teriyaki Wingettes 22
Wingettes in Honey Sauce. 23
Spicy Franks. 24
Bubbly Franks. 24

Unbelievable Crab Dip

1 (6 ounce) can white
   crabmeat, drained,
   flaked   2 (170 g)
1 (8 ounce) package
   cream cheese,
   softened   230 g
½ cup (1 stick) butter,
   sliced   115 g
2 tablespoons white
   cooking wine   30 ml

- Combine crabmeat, cream cheese, butter and wine in small, sprayed slow cooker.

- Cover and cook on LOW for 1 hour and gently stir to combine all ingredients. Serve from cooker with chips or crackers. Serves 4 to 6.

Crab Dip

1 (8 ounce) and
   1 (3 ounce)
   packages cream
   cheese, softened   230 g/85 g
⅔ cup mayonnaise   150 g
1 tablespoon marinade
   for chicken
   (Lea & Perrins)   15 ml
1 tablespoon sherry
   or cooking sherry   15 ml
3 fresh green onions
   with tops, chopped
2 (6 ounce) cans
   crabmeat,
   drained, flaked   2 (170 g)

- Combine cream cheese, mayonnaise, 1 teaspoon (5 ml) salt and Worcestershire in bowl and mix well with fork.

- Stir in sherry, onions and crabmeat and spoon into small, sprayed slow cooker.

- Cover and cook on LOW for 1 hour 30 minutes to 2 hours and stir once. Serves 6 to 8.

Broccoli Dip

¾ cup (1½ sticks) butter   170 g
2 cups thinly sliced celery   200 g
1 onion, finely chopped
3 tablespoons flour   20 g
1 (10 ounce) can cream of
    chicken soup   280 g
1 (10 ounce) box chopped
    broccoli, thawed   280 g
1 (5 ounce) garlic cheese
    roll, cut in chunks   145 g

- Wheat crackers or corn chips

- Melt butter in skillet and saute celery and onion, but do not brown; stir in flour.

- Spoon into small slow cooker, stir in remaining ingredients and mix well.

- Cover and cook on LOW for 2 to 3 hours and stir several times.

- Serve with wheat crackers or corn chips. Serves 6 to 8.

Hot Southwest Dip

1½ pounds lean ground
    beef   680 g
2 onions, finely diced
1 (10 ounce) can diced
    tomatoes and green
    chilies   280 g
1 (8 ounce) can tomato
    sauce   230 g
2 (16 ounce) packages
    shredded Mexican
    Velveeta cheese   455 g
Tortilla chips

- Cook beef and onions in large skillet until onions are translucent. Drain and transfer to sprayed slow cooker. Add tomatoes and green chilies, tomato sauce and cheese; stir until they blend well.

- Cover and cook on LOW for 2 hours, stirring every 30 minutes. Use chips for dipping. Serves 12 to 14.

Cheesy Bacon Dip

2 (8 ounce) packages
  cream cheese,
  softened   2 (230 g)
1 (8 ounce) package
  shredded colby
  Jack cheese   230 g
2 tablespoons
  mustard   30 ml
2 teaspoons marinade
  for chicken
  (Lea & Perrins)   30 g
4 fresh green onions
  with tops, sliced
1 pound bacon,
  cooked, crumbled 455 g
Rye or pumpernickel
  bread

- Cut cream cheese into cubes and place in 4 to 5-quart (4 to 5 L) slow cooker.

- Add colby Jack cheese, mustard, white Worcestershire, green onions and ¼ teaspoon (1 ml) salt.

- Cover and cook on LOW for 1 hour and stir to melt cheese.

- Stir in crumbled bacon. Serve with small-size rye bread or toasted pumpernickel bread. Serves 6 to 8.

Hamburger Dip

Men love this meaty, spicy dip.

2 pounds lean ground beef	910 g
2 tablespoons dried minced onion	30 ml
1½ teaspoons dried oregano leaves	7 ml
1 tablespoon chili powder	15 ml
2 teaspoons sugar	10 ml
1 (10 ounce) can tomatoes and green chilies	280 g
½ cup chili sauce	135 g
2 (16 ounce) packages cubed Mexican Velveeta® cheese	2 (455 g)
Chips or crackers	

- Brown ground beef in large skillet, drain and transfer to sprayed 4 to 5-quart (4 to 5 L) slow cooker.

- Add remaining ingredients plus ½ to 1 cup (125 to 250 ml) water and stir well.

- Cover and cook on LOW for 1 hour 30 minutes to 2 hours. Stir once or twice during cooking time. Add a little salt, if desired. Serve hot with chips or spread on crackers. Serves 8 to 10.

Hot Broccoli Dip

1 (16 ounce) box Mexican
    Velveeta® cheese,
    cubed   455 g
1 (10 ounce) can golden
    mushroom soup   280 g
¼ cup milk   60 ml
1 (10 ounce) box frozen
    chopped broccoli,
    thawed   280 g

- Combine cheese, soup and milk in sprayed slow cooker, stir well and fold in broccoli.

- Cover and cook on LOW for 1 to 2 hours. Stir before serving. Serves 8 to 10.

Indian-Corn Dip

1 pound lean ground
    beef   455 g
1 onion, finely chopped
1 (15 ounce) can whole
    kernel corn, drained 425 g
1 (16 ounce) jar salsa 455 g
1 (1 pound) package
    cubed Velveeta®
    cheese   455 g
Tortilla chips

- Brown and cook beef in skillet on low heat for about 10 minutes and drain.

- Transfer to slow cooker and add onion, corn, salsa and cheese.

- Cover and cook on LOW for 1 hour, remove lid and stir. Serve with tortilla chips. Serves 6 to 8.

Chicken-Enchilada Dip

2 pounds boneless,
   skinless chicken
   thighs, cubed   910 g
1 (10 ounce) can
   enchilada sauce   280 g
1 (7 ounce) can
   chopped green
   chilies, drained   195 g
1 small onion, finely
   chopped
1 large red bell
   pepper, seeded,
   finely chopped
2 (8 ounce) packages
   cream cheese,
   cubed   2 (230 g)
1 (16 ounce) package
   shredded
   American cheese 455 g
Tortilla chips

- Place chicken thighs, enchilada sauce, green chilies, onion and bell pepper in sprayed 4 to 5-quart (4 to 5 L) slow cooker.

- Cover and cook on LOW for 4 to 6 hours. Stir in cream cheese and American cheese and cook an additional 30 minutes.

- Stir several times during cooking. Serve with tortilla chips. Serves 8 to 10.

Pepperoni Dip

1 (6 ounce) package
    pepperoni   170 g
1 bunch fresh green
    onions, thinly sliced
½ red bell pepper, finely
    chopped
1 medium tomato, finely
    chopped
1 (14 ounce) jar pizza
    sauce   400 g
1½ cups shredded
    mozzarella
    cheese   170 g
1 (8 ounce) package
    cream cheese, cubed   230 g
Wheat crackers or
    tortilla chips

- Chop pepperoni into small pieces and place in small slow cooker.

- Add onion, bell pepper, tomato and pizza sauce and stir well.

- Cover and cook on LOW for 2 hours 30 minutes to 3 hours 30 minutes.

- Stir in mozzarella and cream cheese and stir until they melt.

- Serve with wheat crackers or tortilla chips. Serves 4 to 6.

Sausage-Hamburger Dip

1 pound bulk pork	
sausage	455 g
1 pound lean ground	
beef	455 g
1 cup hot salsa	265 g
1 (10 ounce) can	
cream of	
mushroom soup	280 g
1 (10 ounce) can	
tomatoes and	
green chilies	280 g
1 teaspoon garlic	
powder	5 ml
¾ teaspoon ground	
oregano	4 ml
2 (16 ounce) packages	
cubed Velveeta®	
cheese	2 (455 g)

- Cook sausage and ground beef in large skillet for 15 minutes and drain.

- Place in sprayed 4 to 5-quart (4 to 5 L) slow cooker.

- Add salsa, mushroom soup, tomatoes and green chilies, garlic powder and oregano; stir well. Fold in cheese.

- Cover and cook on LOW for 1 hour or until cheese melts. Stir once during cooking time.

- Serve from cooker. Serves 8 to 10.

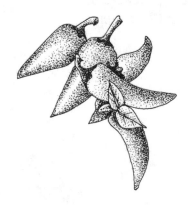

Whiz Bang Dip

1 pound lean ground
   beef   455 g
1 small onion, very
   finely chopped
2 (16 ounce) package
   cubed Velveeta®
   cheese   2 (455 g)
2 (10 ounce) cans
   chopped tomatoes
   and green chilies   2 (280 g)
1 teaspoon minced
   garlic   5 ml
Tortilla chips

- Cook beef in skillet on low heat for 10 minutes and break up large meat chunks. Transfer to 4-quart (4 L) slow cooker and add onion, cheese, tomatoes and green chilies, and garlic.

- Stir well, cover and cook on LOW for 1 hour. Serve with tortilla chips. Serves 6 to 8.

The Big Dipper

2 (15 ounce) cans
   chili   2 (425 g)
1 (10 ounce) can
   tomatoes and
   green chilies   280 g
1 (16 ounce) package
   cubed Velveeta®
   cheese   455 g
1 bunch fresh green
   onions, chopped

- Place all ingredients in slow cooker. Cover and cook on LOW for 1 hour to 1 hour 30 minutes.

- Serve right from slow cooker. Stir before serving. Serves 6 to 8.

Firecrackers and Bacon

1 (16 ounce) package cubed
   Mexican Velveeta®
   cheese   455 g
1 (10 ounce) can tomatoes
   and green chilies   280 g
1 tablespoon dry minced
   onion   15 ml
2 teaspoons
   Worcestershire sauce 10 ml
½ teaspoon dried
   mustard   2 ml
½ cup whipping cream
   or half-and-half
   cream   125 ml
16 slices bacon, cooked,
   crumbled, divided

- Combine cubed cheese, tomatoes and green chilies, onion, Worcestershire, mustard and cream to small, sprayed slow cooker.

- Turn heat to LOW, cover and cook for about 1 hour, stirring several times to make sure cheese melts.

- While cheese is melting, place bacon in skillet, fry, drain and crumble.

- Fold three-fourths of bacon into cheese mixture. When ready to "dip", sprinkle remaining bacon on top and serve from slow cooker. Serves 4 to 6.

Great Balls of Fire

1 pound hot sausage	455 g
1 (10 ounce) can chopped tomatoes and green chilies	280 g
1 (2 pound) box Velveeta® cheese	910 g

- Brown and cook sausage in skillet, drain and place in small, sprayed slow cooker.

- Stir in tomatoes and green chilies and mix well.

- Cut cheese into chunks and add to sausage-tomato mixture.

- Cover and cook on LOW for 1 hour or until cheese melts.

- Stir when ready to serve and serve hot in slow cooker. Serves 4 to 6.

TIP: *This works best with large tortilla chips.*

Hot Reuben Spread

1 (8 ounce) package shredded Swiss cheese	230 g
¾ cup drained sauerkraut, rinsed, drained	110 g
1 (8 ounce) package cream cheese, softened, cubed	230 g
2 (2.5 ounce) packages sliced corned beef, chopped	2 (70 g)

- Combine Swiss cheese, sauerkraut, cream cheese and corned beef in bowl and spoon into small, sprayed slow cooker.

- Cover and cook on LOW for 1 hour.

- Serve on slices of 3-inch (8 cm) rye bread. Serves 4 to 6.

Crab-Artichoke Spread

1 (6 ounce) can crabmeat,
   flaked   170 g
½ cup grated parmesan
   cheese   50 g
1 bunch fresh green
   onions, sliced
1½ tablespoons lemon
   juice   22 ml
1 (15 ounce) can artichoke
   hearts, drained, finely
   chopped   425 g
1 (8 ounce) package
   cream cheese, cubed   230 g

- Toasted bagel chips

- Combine all ingredients in small, sprayed slow cooker and stir well.

- Cover and cook on LOW for 1 hour to 1 hour 30 minutes. Stir until cream cheese mixes well. Serve on toasted bagel chips. Serves 4 to 6.

Party Smokies

1 cup ketchup   270 g
1 cup plum jelly   320 g
1 tablespoon lemon
   juice   15 ml
2 (5 ounce) packages
   tiny smoked
   sausages   2 (145 g)

- Combine all ingredients in small, sprayed slow cooker.

- Cover and cook on LOW for 1 hour.

- Stir before serving. Serve right from cooker. Serves 4 to 6.

Sausage-Pineapple Bits

The "sweet and hot" makes a delicious combo.

1 (1 pound) link cooked Polish sausage, skinned	455 g
1 (1 pound) hot bulk sausage	455 g
1 (8 ounce) can crushed pineapple with juice	230 g
1 cup apricot preserves	320 g
1 tablespoon marinade for chicken (Lea & Perrins)	15 ml
1½ cups packed brown sugar	330 g

- Slice link sausage into ½-inch (1.2 cm) pieces. Shape bulk sausage into 1-inch (2.5 cm) balls and brown in skillet.

- Combine sausage pieces, sausage balls, pineapple, apricot preserves, Worcestershire sauce and brown sugar in slow cooker. Stir gently so meatballs do not break up.

- Cover and cook on LOW for 1 hour 30 minutes to 2 hours. Serves 8 to 10.

Teriyaki Wingettes

2½ pounds chicken wingettes	**1.1 kg**
1 onion, chopped	
1 cup soy sauce	**250 ml**
1 cup packed brown sugar	**220 g**
1 teaspoon minced garlic	**5 ml**
1½ teaspoons ground ginger	**7 ml**

- Rinse chicken and pat dry. Place chicken wingettes on broiler pan and broil for about 10 minutes on both sides.

- Transfer wingettes to large slow cooker.

- Combine onion, soy sauce, brown sugar, garlic and ginger in bowl. Spoon sauce over wingettes.

- Cover and cook on HIGH for 2 hours. Stir wingettes once during cooking to coat chicken evenly with sauce. Serves 8 to 10.

Wingettes in Honey Sauce

1 (2 pound) package
    chicken wingettes   **910 g**
2 cups honey   **680 g**
¾ cup soy sauce   **175 ml**
¾ cup chili sauce   **205 g**
¼ cup canola oil   **60 ml**
1 teaspoon minced
    garlic   **5 ml**
Dried parsley flakes

- Rinse chicken, pat dry and sprinkle with a little salt and pepper.

- Place wingettes in broiler pan and broil for 20 minutes (10 minutes on each side) or until light brown.

- Transfer to sprayed slow cooker.

- Combine honey, soy sauce, chili sauce, oil and garlic in bowl and spoon over wingettes.

- Cover and cook on LOW for 4 to 5 hours or on HIGH for 2 hours to 2 hours 30 minutes. Garnish with dried parsley flakes, if desired. Serves 8 to 10.

Spicy Franks

1 cup packed brown	
sugar	220 g
1 cup chili sauce	270 g
1 tablespoon red	
wine vinegar	15 ml
2 teaspoons soy sauce	10 ml
2 teaspoons dijon-	
style mustard	10 ml
2 (12 ounce) packages	
frankfurters	2 (340 g)

- Combine brown sugar, chili sauce, vinegar, soy sauce and mustard in small, sprayed slow cooker and mix well. Cut frankfurters diagonally in 1-inch (2.5 cm) pieces. Stir in frankfurters.

- Cover and cook on LOW for 1 to 2 hours.

- Serve from cooker using cocktail picks. Serves 4.

Bubbly Franks

1 (1 pound) package	
wieners	455 g
½ cup chili sauce	135 g
⅔ cup packed brown	
sugar	150 g
½ cup bourbon	125 ml

- Cut wieners diagonally into bite-size pieces. Combine chili sauce, brown sugar and bourbon in small slow cooker.

- Stir in wieners. Cover and cook on LOW for 1 to 2 hours.

- Serve in chafing dish. Serves 6 to 8.

Soup's On!

Soups, Stews,
Chowders & Jambalayas

Soup's On! Contents

Potato Soup Plus! 28
Mexican-Meatball Soup 28
Tasty Chicken and Rice Soup 29
Taco Soup 30
Taco Soup Olé. 31
Taco-Chili Soup 32
Spicy Sausage Soup 33
Tortilla Soup .34
Southern Soup. 35
Saucy Cabbage Soup. 36
Soup with a Zip. 36
Potato and Leek Soup 37
Pork and Hominy Soup 38
Pizza Soup 39
Pasta-Veggie Soup 40
Navy Bean Soup 41
Meatball Soup. 42
Pinto Bean-Vegetable Soup. 43
Delicious Broccoli-Cheese Soup. 43
Italian Bean Soup 44
Ham, Bean and Pasta Soup 45
French Onion Soup 46
Tortellini Soup 47
Enchilada Soup. 48
Hamburger Soup. 49
Tasty Black Bean Soup 49
Sausage-Pizza Soup 50
Turkey and Mushroom Soup 50
Creamy Vegetable Soup 51
Cream of Zucchini Soup 52
Black Bean Soup. 53
Confetti-Chicken Soup 54

Tasty Cabbage and Beef Soup. 55
Chili Soup. 55
Chicken and Rice Soup 56
Chicken and Barley Soup 56
Chicken-Pasta Soup 57
Vegetable-Lentil Soup. 58
Cheesy Potato Soup 58
Turkey-Tortilla Soup. 59
Cheddar Soup Plus 60
Cajun Bean Soup. 60
Black-Eyed Soup 61
Beefy Rice Soup 61
Beef and Black Bean Soup 62
Beef and Noodle Soup 63
Beef and Barley Soup 64
Beans and Barley Soup 64
Beans 'n Sausage Soup 65
Minestrone Soup. 66
Chicken-Tortellini Stew 66
Winter Minestrone 67
Pancho Villa Stew. 68
A Different Stew. 69
Chicken Stew 69
Southern Ham Stew 70
Serious Bean Stew 71
Santa Fe Stew 72
Pork-Vegetable Stew. 73
Roast and Vegetable Stew 74
Olé! For Stew. 74
Meatball Stew. 75
Meatball and Veggie Stew. 75
Italian-Vegetable Stew 76

Soup's On! Contents

Hungarian Stew. 76

Hearty Meatball Stew 77

Ham and Cabbage Stew 77

South-of-the-Border Beef Stew. 78

Comfort Stew 79

Chicken Stew over Biscuits. 80

White Lightning Chili. 81

Vegetarian Chili 82

Vegetable Chili 83

Traditional Chili 84

Turkey-Veggie Chili 85

Easy Chili 86

Chunky Chili. 87

Ham-Vegetable Chowder 88

Crab Chowder. 89

Country Chicken Chowder 90

Chicken Chowder 91

Oyster Chowder 92

Split-Pea and Ham Chowder. 92

Corn-Ham Chowder 93

Shrimp and Ham Jambalaya 94

Shrimp and Sausage Jambalaya. 95

Shrimp and Chicken Jambalaya 96

Potato Soup Plus!

5 medium potatoes,
  peeled, cubed
2 cups cooked, cubed
  ham   280 g
1 cup fresh broccoli
  florets, cut very,
  very fine   70 g
1 (10 ounce) can cheddar
  cheese soup   280 g
1 (10 ounce) can fiesta
  nacho cheese soup   280 g
1 (14 ounce) can chicken
  broth   400 g
2½ soup cans milk
Paprika

- Place potatoes, ham and broccoli in sprayed slow cooker.

- Combine soups and milk in saucepan. Heat just enough to mix until smooth. Stir into ingredients already in slow cooker.

- Cover and cook on LOW for 7 to 9 hours.

- When serving, sprinkle a little paprika over each serving. Serves 6 to 8.

Mexican-Meatball Soup

3 (14 ounce) cans
  beef broth   3 (400 g)
1 (16 ounce) jar hot
  salsa   455 g
1 (16 ounce) package
  frozen whole
  kernel corn,
  thawed   455 g
1 (16 ounce) package
  frozen meatballs,
  thawed   455 g
1 teaspoon minced
  garlic   5 ml

- Combine all ingredients in slow cooker and stir well.

- Cover and cook on LOW for 5 to 7 hours. Serves 6 to 8.

Tasty Chicken and Rice Soup

1 pound boneless, skinless chicken breasts	455 g
½ cup brown rice	95 g
1 (10 ounce) can cream of chicken soup	280 g
1 (10 ounce) can cream of celery soup	280 g
1 (14 ounce) can chicken broth with roasted garlic	400 g
1 (16 ounce) package frozen sliced carrots, thawed	455 g
1 cup half-and-half cream	250 ml

- Cut chicken into 1-inch pieces. Place pieces in sprayed 4 to 5-quart (4 to 5 L) slow cooker.

- Combine and mix rice, soups, chicken broth and carrots in bowl and pour over chicken.

- Cover and cook on LOW 7 to 8 hours.

- Turn heat to HIGH, add half-and-half cream and cook an additional 15 to 20 minutes. Serves 6 to 8.

Taco Soup

1½ pounds lean ground beef	680 g
1 (1 ounce) packet taco seasoning	30 g
2 (15 ounce) cans Mexican stewed tomatoes	2 (425 g)
2 (15 ounce) cans chili beans with liquid	2 (425g)
1 (15 ounce) can whole kernel corn, drained	425 g
Crushed tortilla chips	
Shredded cheddar cheese	

- Brown ground beef in skillet until it is no longer pink. Place in 5 to 6-quart (5 to 6 L) slow cooker.

- Add taco seasoning, tomatoes, chili beans, corn and 1 cup (250 ml) water and mix well.

- Cover and cook on LOW for 4 hours or on HIGH for 1 to 2 hours.

- Serve over crushed tortilla chips and sprinkle some shredded cheddar cheese over top of each serving. Serves 6 to 8.

Taco Soup Olé

2 pounds lean ground beef	910 g
2 (15 ounce) cans ranch-style beans with liquid	2 (425 g)
1 (15 ounce) can whole kernel corn, drained	425 g
2 (15 ounce) cans stewed tomatoes	2 (425 g)
1 (10 ounce) can tomatoes and green chilies	280 g
1 (.04 ounce) packet ranch dressing mix	10 g
1 (1 ounce) packet taco seasoning	30 g
Shredded cheddar cheese	

- Brown ground beef in large skillet, drain and transfer to slow cooker.

- Add remaining ingredients and stir well.

- Cover and cook on LOW for 8 to 10 hours.

- When serving, sprinkle cheese over each serving. Serve 6 to 8.

Taco-Chili Soup

2 pounds very lean
   stew meat   910 g
2 (15 ounce) cans
   Mexican stewed
   tomatoes   2 (425 g)
1 (1 ounce) packet
   taco seasoning
   mix   30 g
2 (15 ounce) cans
   pinto beans with
   liquid   2 (425 g)
1 (15 ounce) can
   whole kernel corn
   with liquid   425 g
Green onions,
   chopped

- Cut large pieces of stew meat in half and brown in large skillet.

- Combine stew meat, tomatoes, taco seasoning mix, beans, corn and ¾ cup (175 ml) water in 4 to 5-quart (4 to 5 L) slow cooker. (If you are not into "spicy", use original recipe stewed tomatoes instead of Mexican.)

- Cover and cook on LOW for 5 to 7 hours. Garnish each serving with chopped green onions. Serves 6 to 8.

Spicy Sausage Soup

1 pound mild bulk sausage	455 g
1 pound hot bulk sausage	455 g
2 (15 ounce) cans Mexican stewed tomatoes	2 (425 g)
3 cups chopped celery	305 g
1 cup sliced carrots	120 g
1 (15 ounce) can cut green beans, drained	425 g
1 (14 ounce) can chicken broth	400 g
1 teaspoon seasoned salt	5 ml

- Combine mild and hot sausage, shape into small balls and place in non-stick skillet. Brown thoroughly and drain.

- Place in large, sprayed slow cooker.

- Add remaining ingredients plus 1 cup (250 ml) water and stir gently so meatballs will not break-up.

- Cover and cook on LOW 6 to 7 hours. Serves 6 to 8.

Tortilla Soup

3 large boneless, skinless
  chicken breast halves,
  cubed
1 (10 ounce) package
  frozen whole
  kernel corn,
  thawed   280 g
1 onion, chopped
3 (14 ounce) cans
  chicken broth   3 (400 g)
1 (6 ounce) can
  tomato paste   170 g
2 (10 ounce) cans
  tomatoes and
  green chilies   2 (280 g)
2 teaspoons
  ground cumin   10 ml
1 teaspoon chili
  powder   5 ml
1 teaspoon minced
  garlic   5 ml
6 corn tortillas

- Combine chicken cubes, corn, onion, broth, tomato paste, tomatoes and green chilies, cumin, chili powder, 1 teaspoon (5 ml) salt and garlic in large slow cooker.

- Cover and cook on LOW for 5 to 7 hours or on HIGH for 3 hours to 3 hours 30 minutes.

- Preheat oven to 375° (190° C).

- While soup is cooking, cut tortillas into ¼-inch (6 mm) strips and place on baking sheet.

- Bake for about 5 minutes or until crisp.

- Serve baked tortilla strips with soup. Serves 6 to 8.

Southern Soup

1½ cups dried black-eyed peas	360 g
2 - 3 cups cooked, cubed ham	280 - 420 g
1 (15 ounce) can whole kernel corn	425 g
1 (10 ounce) package frozen cut okra, thawed	280 g
1 onion, chopped	
1 large potato, cut into small cubes	
2 teaspoons Cajun seasoning	10 ml
1 (14 ounce) can chicken broth	400 g
2 (15 ounce) cans Mexican stewed tomatoes	2 (425 g)

- Rinse peas and drain. Combine peas and 5 cups (1.2 L) water in large saucepan.

- Bring to a boil, reduce heat, simmer for about 10 minutes and drain.

- Combine peas, ham, corn, okra, onion, potato, seasoning, broth and 2 cups (500 ml) water in 5 to 6-quart (5 to 6 L) slow cooker.

- Cover and cook on LOW for 6 to 8 hours.

- Add stewed tomatoes and continue cooking for an additional 1 hour. Serves 6 to 8.

Saucy Cabbage Soup

1 pound lean ground beef	455 g
1 small head cabbage, chopped	
2 (15 ounce) cans jalapeno pinto beans with liquid	2 (425 g)
1 (15 ounce) can tomato sauce	425 g
1 (15 ounce) can Mexican stewed tomatoes	425 g
1 (14 ounce) can beef broth	400 g
2 teaspoons ground cumin	10 ml

- Brown ground beef in skillet, drain and place in 5 to 6-quart (5 to 6 L) slow cooker.

- Add cabbage, beans, tomato sauce, tomatoes, broth, cumin and 1 cup (250 ml) water and mix well.

- Cover and cook on LOW for 5 to 6 hours or until cabbage is tender. Serves 4 to 6.

Soup with a Zip

2 (15 ounce) cans Mexican stewed tomatoes	2 (425 g)
2 (14 ounce) cans chicken broth	2 (400 g)
2 (10 ounce) cans chicken noodle soup	2 (280 g)
1 (15 ounce) can shoe-peg corn, drained	425 g
1 (15 ounce) can cut green beans, drained	425 g
Shredded pepper-Jack cheese	

- Place all ingredients except cheese in 4 to 5-quart (4 to 5 L) slow cooker and mix well.

- Cover and cook on LOW for 2 to 3 hours. When ready to serve, sprinkle shredded cheese over each bowl of soup. Serves 4 to 6.

Potato and Leek Soup

1 (1 ounce) packet white sauce mix	30 g
1 (28 ounce) package frozen hash-brown potatoes with onions and peppers	795 g
3 medium leeks, sliced	
3 cups cooked, cubed ham	420 g
1 (12 ounce) can evaporated milk	340 g
1 (8 ounce) carton sour cream	230 g

- Pour 3 cups (750 ml) water in 4 to 5-quart (4 to 5 L) slow cooker and stir white sauce until smooth.

- Add hash-brown potatoes, leeks, ham and evaporated milk.

- Cover and cook on LOW for 7 to 9 hours or on HIGH for 3 hours 30 minutes to 4 hours 30 minutes.

- When ready to serve, turn heat to HIGH. Take out about 2 cups (500 ml) hot soup and pour into separate bowl. Stir in sour cream and return to cooker.

- Cover and cook for an additional 15 minutes or until mixture is thoroughly hot. Serves 6 to 8.

Pork and Hominy Soup

2 pounds pork shoulder	910 g
1 onion, chopped	
2 ribs celery, sliced	
2 (15 ounce) cans yellow hominy with liquid	2 (425 g)
2 (15 ounce) cans stewed tomatoes	2 (425 g)
2 (14 ounce) cans chicken broth	2 (400 g)
1½ teaspoons ground cumin	7 ml
Flour tortillas	
Shredded cheese	
Green onions, chopped	

- Cut pork into ½-inch (1.2 cm) cubes.

- Sprinkle pork cubes with a little salt and pepper and brown in skillet.

- Place in 5 to 6-quart (5 to 6 L) slow cooker.

- Combine onion, celery, hominy, stewed tomatoes, cumin and 1 cup (250 ml) water in bowl.

- Pour over pork cubes.

- Cover and cook on HIGH for 6 to 7 hours.

- Serve with warmed, buttered tortillas and top each bowl of soup with some shredded cheese and chopped green onions. Serves 6 to 8.

Pizza Soup

3 (10 ounce) cans tomato bisque soup	3 (280 g)
1 (10 ounce) can French onion soup	280 g
2 teaspoons Italian seasoning	10 ml
¾ cup tiny pasta shells	80 g
1½ cups shredded mozzarella cheese	170 g

- Combine soups, Italian seasoning and 1½ soup cans water in 4 to 5-quart (4 to 5 L) slow cooker. Cover and cook on HIGH for 1 hour or until mixture is hot.

- Add pasta shells and cook for 1 hour 30 minutes to 2 hours or until pasta is cooked.

- Stir several times to keep pasta from sticking to bottom of slow cooker.

- Turn heat off, add mozzarella cheese and stir until cheese melts. Serves 6 to 8.

TIP: For a special way to serve this soup, sprinkle some french-fried onions over top of each serving.

Pasta-Veggie Soup

2 yellow squash, peeled,
  chopped
2 zucchini, sliced
1 (10 ounce) package
  frozen whole
  kernel corn,
  thawed   280 g
1 red bell pepper,
  chopped
1 (15 ounce) can
  stewed tomatoes   425 g
1 teaspoon Italian
  seasoning   5 ml
2 teaspoons dried
  oregano   10 ml
2 (14 ounce) cans
  beef broth   2 (400 g)
¾ cup small shell
  pasta   80 g
Shredded mozzarella
  cheese

- Combine squash, zucchini, corn, bell pepper, tomatoes, Italian seasoning, oregano, broth and 2 cups (500 ml) water in 6-quart (6 L) slow cooker.

- Cover and cook on LOW for 6 to 7 hours.

- Add pasta shells and cook an additional 30 to 45 minutes or until pasta is tender.

- Garnish with a sprinkle of shredded mozzarella cheese on each bowl of soup. Serves 4 to 5.

Navy Bean Soup

8 slices thick-cut bacon,
   divided
1 carrot
3 (15 ounce) cans
   navy beans with
   liquid   **3 (425 g)**
3 ribs celery, chopped
1 onion, chopped
2 (15 ounce) cans
   chicken broth   **2 (425 g)**
1 teaspoon Italian
   herb seasoning   **5 ml**
1 (10 ounce) can
   cream of chicken
   soup   **280 g**

- Cook bacon in skillet, drain and crumble. (Reserve 2 crumbled slices for garnish.)

- Cut carrot in half lengthwise and slice.

- Combine most of crumbled bacon, carrot, beans, celery, onion, broth, seasoning, 1 cup (250 ml) water in 5 to 6-quart (5 to 6 L) slow cooker and stir to mix.

- Cover and cook on LOW for 5 to 6 hours.

- Ladle 2 cups (500 ml) soup mixture into food processor or blender and process until smooth.

- Return to cooker, add cream of chicken soup and stir to mix.

- Turn heat to HIGH and cook for additional 10 to 15 minutes. Serves 6 to 8.

Meatball Soup

1 (32 ounce) package
   frozen meatballs,
   thawed   910 g
2 (15 ounce) cans
   stewed tomatoes   2 (425 g)
3 large potatoes,
   peeled, diced
4 carrots, peeled,
   sliced
2 medium onions,
   chopped
2 (14 ounce) cans
   beef broth   2 (400 g)
2 tablespoons
   cornstarch   15 g

- Combine meatballs, tomatoes, potatoes, carrots, onions, beef broth, a little salt and pepper and 1 cup (250 ml) water in sprayed 6-quart (6 L) slow cooker.

- Cover and cook on LOW for 5 to 6 hours.

- Turn heat to HIGH and combine cornstarch with ¼ cup (60 ml) water in bowl. Pour into cooker and cook for an additional 10 or 15 minutes or until slightly thick. Serves 4 to 6.

Pinto Bean-Vegetable Soup

4 (15 ounce) cans seasoned pinto beans with liquid	4 (425 g)
1 (10 ounce) package frozen Seasoning Blend chopped onions and peppers	280 g
2 cups chopped celery	200 g
2 (14 ounce) cans chicken broth	2 (400 g)
1 teaspoon Cajun seasoning	5 ml
⅛ teaspoon cayenne pepper	.5 ml

- Place all ingredients plus 1 cup (250 ml) water in 5-quart (5 L) slow cooker and stir well.

- Cover and cook on LOW 5 to 6 hours. Serves 6 to 8.

Delicious Broccoli-Cheese Soup

1 (16 ounce) package frozen chopped broccoli, thawed	455 g
1 (12 ounce) package cubed Velveeta® cheese	340 g
1 (2 ounce) packet white sauce mix	60 g
1 (1 ounce) packet vegetable soup mix	30 g
1 (12 ounce) can evaporated milk	340 g
1 (14 ounce) can chicken broth	400 g

- Combine all ingredients plus 2 cups (500 ml) water in large, sprayed slow cooker and stir well.

- Cover and cook on LOW for 6 to 7 hours or on HIGH for 3 hours 30 minutes to 4 hours.

- Stir for 1 hour before serving time. Serves 4 to 6.

Italian Bean Soup

2 (15 ounce) cans
    great northern
    beans with liquid   2 (425 g)
2 (15 ounce) cans
    pinto beans with
    liquid   2 (425 g)
1 large onion,
    chopped
1 tablespoon instant
    beef bouillon
    granules   15 ml
1 tablespoon minced
    garlic   15 ml
2 teaspoons Italian
    seasoning   10 ml
2 (15 ounce) cans
    Italian stewed
    tomatoes   2 (425 g)
1 (15 ounce) can cut
    green beans,
    drained   425 g

- Combine northern beans, pinto beans, onion, beef bouillon, garlic, Italian seasoning and 2 cups (500 ml) water in large slow cooker.

- Cover and cook on LOW for 6 to 8 hours.

- Turn heat to HIGH, add stewed tomatoes and green beans and stir well.

- Continue cooking for an additional 30 minutes or until green beans are tender. Serves 6 to 8.

*TIP: Serve with crispy
      Italian toast.*

Ham, Bean and Pasta Soup

1 onion, finely chopped	
2 ribs celery, chopped	
2 teaspoons minced garlic	10 ml
2 (14 ounce) cans chicken broth	2 (400 g)
2 (15 ounce) cans pork and beans with liquid	2 (425 g)
3 cups cooked, cubed ham	420 g
⅓ cup pasta shells	35 g
Bacon, cooked	

- Combine onion, celery, garlic, chicken broth, beans, ham and 1 cup (250 ml) water in 5 to 6-quart (5 to 6 L) slow cooker.

- Cover and cook on LOW for 4 to 5 hours.

- Turn cooker to HIGH heat, add pasta and cook for additional 35 to 45 minutes or until pasta is tender.

- Garnish each serving with cooked, crisp and crumbled bacon. Serves 6 to 8.

French Onion Soup

5 - 6 sweet onions,
   thinly sliced
1 clove garlic, minced
2 tablespoons butter   30 g
2 (14 ounce) cans
   beef broth   2 (400 g)
2 teaspoons
   Worcestershire
   sauce   10 ml
6 - 8 (1 inch) slices
   French bread   6 - 8 (2.5 cm)
8 slices Swiss
   cheese

- Cook onions and garlic in large skillet on low heat (DO NOT BROWN) in hot butter for about 20 minutes and stir several times.

- Transfer onion mixture to 4 to 5-quart (4 to 5 L) slow cooker. Add beef broth, Worcestershire and 1 cup (250 ml) water.

- Cover and cook on LOW for 5 to 8 hours or on HIGH for 2 hours 30 minutes to 4 hours.

- Before serving soup, toast bread slices with cheese slice on top. Broil for 3 to 4 minutes or until cheese is light brown and bubbly.

- Ladle soup into bowls and top with toast. Serves 6 to 8.

Tortellini Soup

1 (1 ounce) packet white sauce mix	30 g
3 boneless, skinless chicken breast halves	
1 (14 ounce) can chicken broth	400 g
1 teaspoon minced garlic	5 ml
½ teaspoon dried basil	2 ml
½ teaspoon oregano	2 ml
½ teaspoon cayenne pepper	2 ml
1 (8 ounce) package cheese tortellini	230 g
1½ cups half-and-half cream	375 ml
6 cups fresh baby spinach	180 g

- Place white sauce mix in sprayed 5 to 6-quart (5 to 6 L) slow cooker.

- Stir in 4 cups (1 L) water and stir gradually until mixture is smooth.

- Cut chicken into 1-inch (2.5 cm) pieces. Add chicken, broth, garlic, basil, oregano, cayenne pepper and ½ teaspoon (2 ml) salt to mixture.

- Cover and cook on LOW for 6 to 7 hours or on HIGH for 3 hours.

- Stir in tortellini, cover and cook for additional 1 hour on HIGH.

- Stir in cream and fresh spinach and cook just enough for soup to get hot. Serves 4 to 6.

TIP: Sprinkle a little shredded parmesan cheese on top of each serving.

Enchilada Soup

1 pound lean ground
   beef, browned,
   drained   455 g
1 (15 ounce) can
   Mexican stewed
   tomatoes   425 g
1 (15 ounce) can
   pinto beans
   with liquid   425 g
1 (15 ounce) can
   whole kernel corn
   with liquid   425 g
1 onion, chopped
2 (10 ounce) cans
   enchilada sauce   2 (280 g)
1 (8 ounce) package
   shredded
   4-cheese blend   230 g
Tortilla chips

- Combine beef, tomatoes, beans, corn, onion, enchilada sauce and 1 cup (250 ml) water in sprayed 5 to 6-quart (5 to 6 L) slow cooker and mix well.

- Cover and cook on LOW for 6 to 8 hours or on HIGH for 3 to 4 hours.

- Stir in shredded cheese.

- If desired, top each serving with a few crushed tortilla chips. Serves 6 to 8.

Hamburger Soup

2 pounds lean ground beef	910 g
2 (15 ounce) cans chili without beans	2 (425 g)
1 (16 ounce) package frozen mixed vegetables, thawed	455 g
3 (14 ounce) cans beef broth	3 (400 g)
2 (15 ounce) cans stewed tomatoes	2 (425 g)
1 teaspoon seasoned salt	5 ml

- Brown ground beef in skillet until no longer pink.

- Place in 6-quart (6 L) slow cooker.

- Add chili, vegetables, broth, tomatoes, 1 cup (250 ml) water and seasoned salt and stir well.

- Cover and cook on LOW for 6 to 7 hours. Serves 6 to 8.

Tasty Black Bean Soup

1 pound hot sausage	455 g
1 onion, chopped	
2 (14 ounce) cans chicken broth	2 (400 g)
2 (15 ounce) cans Mexican stewed tomatoes	2 (425 g)
1 green bell pepper, seeded, chopped	
2 (15 ounce) cans black beans, rinsed, drained	2 (425 g)

- Break up sausage and brown with onion in large skillet. Drain off fat and place in large slow cooker.

- Add chicken broth, stewed tomatoes, bell pepper, black beans and 1 cup (250 ml) water. Cover and cook on LOW for 3 to 5 hours. Serves 4 to 6.

Sausage-Pizza Soup

1 (16 ounce) package Italian link sausage, thinly sliced	455 g
1 onion, chopped	
2 (4 ounce) cans sliced mushrooms	2 (115 g)
1 small green bell pepper, cored, seeded, julienned	
1 (15 ounce) can Italian stewed tomatoes	425 g
1 (14 ounce) can beef broth	400 g
1 (8 ounce) can pizza sauce	230 g
Shredded mozzarella cheese	

- Combine all ingredients except cheese in slow cooker and stir well.

- Cover and cook on LOW for 4 to 5 hours.

- Sprinkle mozzarella cheese over each serving. Serves 4 to 6.

Turkey and Mushroom Soup

Another great way to use leftover chicken or turkey

2 cups sliced shitake mushrooms	145 g
2 ribs celery, sliced	
1 small onion, chopped	
2 tablespoons butter	30 g
1 (15 ounce) can sliced carrots	425 g
2 (14 ounce) cans chicken broth	400 g
½ cup orzo pasta	40 g
2 cups cooked, chopped turkey	280 g

- Saute mushrooms, celery and onion in butter in skillet.

- Transfer vegetables to slow cooker and add carrots, broth, orzo and turkey. (Do not use smoked turkey.)

- Cover and cook on LOW for 2 to 3 hours or on HIGH for 1 to 2 hours. Serves 4 to 6.

Creamy Vegetable Soup

3 (14 ounce) cans chicken broth	3 (400 g)
¼ cup (½ stick) butter, melted	60 g
1 (16 ounce) package frozen mixed vegetables	455 g
1 onion, chopped	
3 ribs celery, sliced	
1 teaspoon ground cumin	5 ml
3 zucchini, coarsely chopped	
2 cups chopped, fresh broccoli	480 ml
1 cup half-and-half cream	250 ml

- Combine broth, butter, vegetables, onion, celery, cumin, 1 teaspoon (5 ml) each of salt and pepper in large slow cooker and stir well.

- Cover and cook on LOW for 6 to 7 hours or on HIGH for 3 to 4 hours.

- Stir in zucchini and broccoli. If not using HIGH temperature, turn heat to HIGH and cook an additional 30 minutes to 1 hour or until broccoli is tender-crisp.

- Turn off heat and stir in half-and-half cream. Let stand for 10 minutes before serving. Serves 6 to 8.

Cream of Zucchini Soup

1 small onion, very finely chopped	
3½ - 4 cups grated zucchini with peels	440 - 500 g
2 (14 ounce) cans chicken broth	2 (400 g)
1 teaspoon seasoned salt	5 ml
1 teaspoon dried dill weed	5 ml
½ teaspoon white pepper	2 ml
2 tablespoons butter, melted	30 g
1 (8 ounce) carton sour cream	230 g

- Combine all ingredients except sour cream in small, sprayed slow cooker.

- Cover and cook on LOW for 2 hours.

- Fold in sour cream and continue cooking for about 10 minutes or just until soup is hot. Serves 4.

Black Bean Soup

2 (14 ounce) cans chicken broth	2 (400 g)
3 (15 ounce) cans black beans, rinsed, drained	3 (425 g)
2 (10 ounce) cans tomatoes and green chilies	2 (280 g)
1 onion, chopped	
1 teaspoon ground cumin	5 ml
½ teaspoon dried thyme	2 ml
½ teaspoon dried oregano	2 ml
2 - 3 cups cooked, finely diced ham	280 - 420 g

- Combine chicken broth and black beans in slow cooker and turn cooker to HIGH.

- Cook just long enough for ingredients to get hot.

- Mash about half of beans in cooker.

- Reduce heat to LOW and add tomatoes and green chilies, onion, cumin, thyme, oregano, ham and ¾ cup (175 ml) water.

- Cover and cook for 5 to 6 hours. Serves 6 to 8.

Confetti-Chicken Soup

1 pound boneless,
    skinless chicken
    thighs   455 g
1 (6 ounce) package
    chicken and
    herb-flavored rice   170 g
3 (14 ounce) cans
    chicken broth   3 (400 g)
3 carrots, sliced
1 (10 ounce) can
    cream of chicken
    soup   280 g
1½ tablespoons
    chicken seasoning 22 ml
1 (10 ounce) package
    frozen whole
    kernel corn,
    thawed   280 g
1 (10 ounce) package
    frozen baby green
    peas, thawed   280 g

- Cut thighs in thin strips.

- Combine chicken, rice, chicken broth, carrots, soup, seasoning and 1 cup (250 ml) water in 5 to 6-quart (5 to 6 L) slow cooker.

- Cover and cook on LOW for 8 to 9 hours.

- About 30 minutes before serving, turn heat to HIGH and add corn and peas to cooker. Continue cooking for an additional 30 minutes. Serves 4 to 6.

Tasty Cabbage and Beef Soup

1 pound lean ground beef	455 g
1 (16 ounce) package coleslaw mix	455 g
1 (15 ounce) can cut green beans	425 g
1 (15 ounce) can whole kernel corn	425 g
2 (15 ounce) cans Italian stewed tomatoes	2 (425 g)
2 (14 ounce) cans beef broth	2 (400 g)
Cornbread	

- Brown ground beef in skillet, drain fat and place in large slow cooker.

- Add slaw mix, green beans, corn, tomatoes and beef broth and add a little salt and pepper.

- Cover and cook on LOW for 7 to 9 hours. Serve with cornbread. Serves 6 to 8.

Chili Soup

3 (15 ounce) cans chili with beans	3 (425 g)
1 (15 ounce) can whole kernel corn	425 g
1 (14 ounce) can beef broth	400 g
2 (15 ounce) cans Mexican stewed tomatoes	2 (425 g)
2 teaspoons ground cumin	10 ml
2 teaspoons chili powder	10 ml
Flour tortillas	

- Combine chili, corn, broth, tomatoes, cumin, chili powder and 1 cup (250 ml) water in 5 to 6-quart (5 to 6 L) slow cooker.

- Cover and cook on LOW for 4 to 5 hours. Serve with warm, buttered flour tortillas. Serves 6 to 8.

Chicken and Rice Soup

1 (6 ounce) package long grain-wild rice mix	170 g
1 (1 ounce) packet chicken noodle soup mix	30 g
2 (10 ounce) cans cream of chicken soup	2 (280 g)
2 ribs celery, chopped	
1 - 2 cups cooked, cubed chicken	140 - 280 g

- Combine rice mix, noodle soup mix, chicken soup, celery, chicken and about 6 cups (1.4 L) water in 5 to 6-quart (5 to 6 L) slow cooker.

- Cover and cook on LOW for 2 to 3 hours. Serves 4 to 6.

Chicken and Barley Soup

1½ - 2 pounds boneless, skinless chicken thighs	680 - 910 g
1 (16 ounce) package frozen stew vegetables	455 g
1 (1 ounce) packet vegetable soup mix	30 g
1¼ cups pearl barley	250 g
2 (14 ounce) cans chicken broth	2 (400 g)
1 teaspoon white pepper	5 ml

- Combine all ingredients with 1 teaspoon (5 ml) salt and 4 cups (1 L) water in large, sprayed slow cooker.

- Cover and cook on LOW for 5 to 6 hours or on HIGH for 3 hours. Serves 6 to 8.

Chicken-Pasta Soup

1½ pounds boneless, skinless chicken thighs, cubed	680 g
1 onion, chopped	
3 carrots, sliced	
½ cup halved, pitted ripe olives	65 g
1 teaspoon minced garlic	5 ml
3 (14 ounce) cans chicken broth	3 (400 g)
1 (15 ounce) can Italian stewed tomatoes	425 g
1 teaspoon Italian seasoning	5 ml
½ cup small shell pasta	55 g
Parmesan cheese	

- Combine all ingredients except shell pasta and parmesan cheese in slow cooker.

- Cover and cook on LOW for 8 to 9 hours. About 30 minutes before serving, add pasta and stir.

- Increase heat to HIGH and cook for additional 20 to 30 minutes. Garnish with parmesan cheese. Serves 6 to 8.

Vegetable-Lentil Soup

2 (19 ounce) cans lentil home-style soup	2 (540 g)
1 (15 ounce) can stewed tomatoes	425 g
1 (14 ounce) can chicken broth	400 g
1 onion, chopped	
1 green bell pepper, chopped	
3 ribs celery, sliced	
1 carrot, halved lengthwise, sliced	
2 teaspoons minced garlic	10 ml
1 teaspoon dried marjoram leaves	5 ml

- Combine all ingredients in slow cooker and stir well.

- Cover and cook on LOW for 5 to 6 hours. Serves 6 to 8.

Cheesy Potato Soup

6 medium potatoes, peeled, cubed	
1 onion, very finely chopped	
2 (14 ounce) cans chicken broth	2 (400 g)
½ teaspoon white pepper	2 ml
1 (8 ounce) package shredded American cheese	230 g
1 cup half-and-half cream	250 ml

- Combine potatoes, onion, chicken broth and white pepper in slow cooker.

- Cover and cook on LOW for 8 to 10 hours. Mash potatoes in slow cooker.

- About 1 hour before serving, stir in cheese and cream and cook an additional 1 hour. Serves 4 to 6.

Turkey-Tortilla Soup

This is great for leftover turkey.

2 (14 ounce) cans chicken broth	2 (400 g)
2 (15 ounce) cans Mexican stewed tomatoes	2 (425 g)
1 (16 ounce) package frozen succotash, thawed	455 g
2 teaspoons chili powder	10 ml
1 teaspoon dried cilantro	5 ml
2 cups crushed tortilla chips, divided	110 g
2½ cups cooked, chopped turkey	350 g

- Combine broth, tomatoes, succotash, chili powder, cilantro, ⅓ cup (19 g) crushed tortilla chips and turkey in large slow cooker and stir well.

- Cover and cook on LOW for 3 to 5 hours.

- When ready to serve, sprinkle remaining chips over each serving. Serves 6 to 8.

TIP: Do not use smoked turkey.

Cheddar Soup Plus

2 cups milk	500 ml
1 (7 ounce) package cheddar-broccoli soup starter	200 g
1 cup cooked, finely chopped chicken breasts	140 g
1 (10 ounce) frozen green peas, thawed	280 g
Shredded cheddar cheese	

- Place 5 cups (1.2 L) water and milk in slow cooker. Set heat on HIGH until water and milk come to a boil.

- Stir contents of soup starter into hot water and milk and stir well. Add chopped chicken, green peas and a little salt and pepper.

- Cover and cook on LOW for 2 to 3 hours.

- To serve, sprinkle cheddar cheese over each serving of soup. Serves 4.

Cajun Bean Soup

1 (20 ounce) package Cajun-flavored, 16-bean soup mix with flavor packet	570 g
2 cups cooked, finely chopped ham	280 g
1 chopped onion	
2 (15 ounce) cans stewed tomatoes	2 (425 g)
Cornbread	

- Soak beans overnight in large slow cooker. After soaking, drain water and cover with 2 inches water over beans.

- Cover and cook on LOW for 5 to 6 hours or until beans are tender.

- Add ham, onion, stewed tomatoes and flavor packet in bean soup mix.

- Cover and cook on HIGH for 30 to 45 minutes.

- Serve with cornbread. Serves 4 to 6.

Black-Eyed Soup

5 slices thick-cut bacon,
  diced
1 onion, chopped
1 green bell pepper,
  chopped
3 ribs celery, sliced
3 (15 ounce) cans
  jalapeno black-eyed
  peas with liquid   3 (425 g)
2 (15 ounce) cans
  stewed tomatoes
  with liquid   2 (425 g)
1 teaspoon chicken
  seasoning   5 ml

- Cook bacon pieces in skillet until crisp, drain on paper towel and place in slow cooker.

- With bacon drippings in skillet, saute onion and bell peppers, but do not brown.

- Add onions, bell pepper, celery, black-eyed peas, stewed tomatoes, 1½ cups (375 ml) water and chicken seasoning to slow cooker.

- Cover and cook on LOW for 3 to 4 hours. Serves 6 to 8.

Beefy Rice Soup

1 pound lean beef
  stew meat   455 g
1 (14 ounce) can beef
  broth   400 g
1 (7 ounce) box
  beef-flavored rice
  and vermicelli mix   200 g
1 (10 ounce) package
  frozen peas and
  carrots   280 g
2½ cups vegetable juice   625 ml

- Sprinkle stew meat with seasoned pepper, brown in non-stick skillet, drain and place in large slow cooker.

- Add broth, rice and vermicelli mix, peas and carrots, vegetable juice and 2 cups (500 ml) water.

- Cover and cook on LOW for 6 to 7 hours. Serves 4 to 6.

Beef and Black Bean Soup

1 pound lean ground beef	455 g
2 onions, chopped	
2 cups sliced celery	480 ml
2 (14 ounce) cans beef broth	2 (400 g)
1 (15 ounce) can Mexican stewed tomatoes	425 g
2 (15 ounce) cans black beans, rinsed, drained	2 (425 g)

- Brown beef in skillet until no longer pink. Place in 5 to 6-quart (5 to 6 L) slow cooker.

- Add onions, celery, broth, tomatoes, black beans, ¾ cup (175 ml) water plus a little salt and pepper.

- Cover and cook on LOW for 6 to 7 hours or on HIGH for 3 hours to 3 hours 30 minutes. Serves 6 to 8.

TIP: If you like a zestier soup, add 1 teaspoon (5 ml) chili powder.

Beef and Noodle Soup

1½ pounds lean ground beef	680 g
1 onion, chopped	
2 (15 ounce) cans mixed vegetables, drained	2 (425 g)
2 (15 ounce) cans Italian stewed tomatoes	2 (425 g)
2 (14 ounce) cans beef broth	2 (400 g)
1 teaspoon dried oregano	5 ml
1 cup medium egg noodles	75 g

- Brown and cook ground beef in skillet until no longer pink and transfer to slow cooker.

- Add onion, mixed vegetables, stewed tomatoes, beef broth and oregano.

- Cover and cook on LOW for 4 to 5 hours.

- Cook noodles according to package direction.

- Add noodles to slow cooker and cook for an additional 30 minutes. Serves 4 to 6.

Beef and Barley Soup

1 pound lean ground beef	455 g
3 (14 ounce) cans beef broth	3 (400 g)
¾ cup quick-cooking barley	150 g
3 cups sliced carrots	365 g
2 cups sliced celery	200 g
2 teaspoons beef seasoning	10 ml

- Brown ground beef in skillet, drain and transfer to 5-quart (5 L) slow cooker.

- Add beef broth, barley, carrots, celery and beef seasoning. Cover and cook on LOW for 7 to 8 hours. Serves 4.

Beans and Barley Soup

2 (15 ounce) cans pinto beans with liquid	2 (425 g)
3 (14 ounce) cans chicken broth	3 (400 g)
½ cup quick-cooking barley	100 g
1 (15 ounce) can Italian stewed tomatoes	425 g

- Combine beans, broth, barley, stewed tomatoes and ½ teaspoon (2 ml) pepper in 6-quart (6 L) slow cooker and stir well.

- Cover and cook on LOW for 4 to 5 hours. Serves 6 to 8.

Beans 'n Sausage Soup

1 pound hot Italian sausage	455 g
1 onion, chopped	
1 (15 ounce) can Italian stewed tomatoes	425 g
2 (5 ounce) cans black beans, rinsed, drained	2 (145 g)
2 (15 ounce) cans navy beans with liquid	2 (425 g)
2 (14 ounce) cans beef broth	2 (400 g)
1 teaspoon minced garlic	5 ml
1 teaspoon dried basil	5 ml

- Cut sausage into ½-inch (1.2 cm) pieces. Brown sausage and onion in skillet, drain and transfer to 5 to 6-quart (5 to 6 L) slow cooker.

- Stir in tomatoes, black beans, navy beans, broth, garlic and basil and mix well. Cover and cook on LOW for 5 to 7 hours. Serves 6 to 8.

Minestrone Soup

2 (15 ounce) cans Italian stewed tomatoes — 2 (425 g)
2 (16 ounce) packages frozen vegetables and pasta seasoned sauce — 2 (455 g)
3 (14 ounce) cans beef broth — 3 (400 g)
2 ribs celery, chopped
2 potatoes, peeled, cubed
1 teaspoon Italian herb seasoning — 5 ml
2 (15 ounce) cans kidney beans, drained, rinsed — 2 (425 g)
2 teaspoons minced garlic — 10 ml

- Combine tomatoes, vegetables, broth, celery, potatoes, seasoning, beans, garlic and 1 cup (250 ml) water in large, sprayed slow cooker and mix well.

- Cover and cook on LOW for 4 to 6 hours. Serves 8 to 10.

Chicken-Tortellini Stew

1 (9 ounce) package refrigerated cheese-filled tortellini — 255 g
2 medium yellow squash, halved, sliced
1 red bell pepper, seeded, coarsely chopped
1 onion, chopped
2 (14 ounce) cans chicken broth — 2 (400 g)
1 teaspoon dried rosemary — 5 ml
½ teaspoon dried basil — 2 ml
2 cups cooked, chopped chicken — 280 g

- Place tortellini, squash, bell pepper and onion in slow cooker. Stir in broth, rosemary, basil and chicken.

- Cover and cook on LOW for 2 to 4 hours or until tortellini and vegetables are tender. Serves 4.

Winter Minestrone

1 pound Italian sausage links	455 g
2 medium potatoes, peeled	
2 medium fennel bulbs, trimmed	
2½ cups butternut or acorn squash	285 g
1 onion, chopped	
1 (15 ounce) can kidney beans, rinsed, drained	425 g
2 teaspoons minced garlic	10 ml
1 teaspoon Italian seasoning	5 ml
2 (14 ounce) cans chicken broth	2 (400 g)
1 cup dry white wine	250 ml
3 - 4 cups fresh spinach	90 - 120 g

- Cut sausage, potatoes and fennel into ½-inch (1.2 cm) slices.

- Cook sausage in skillet until brown and drain.

- Combine squash, potatoes, fennel, onion, beans, garlic and Italian seasoning in large slow cooker.

- Top with sausage and pour chicken broth and wine over all.

- Cover and cook on LOW for 7 to 9 hours.

- Stir in spinach, cover and cook for an additional 10 minutes. Serves 6 to 8.

Pancho Villa Stew

3 cups cooked, diced
   ham   **420 g**
1 pound smoked
   sausage   **455 g**
3 (14 ounce) cans
   chicken broth   **3 (400 g)**
1 (15 ounce) can
   diced tomatoes **425 g**
1 (7 ounce) can
   chopped green
   chilies   **200 g**
1 onion, chopped
2 (15 ounce) cans
   pinto beans with
   liquid   **2 (425 g)**
1 (15 ounce) can
   whole kernel corn **425 g**
1 teaspoon garlic
   powder   **5 ml**
2 teaspoons ground
   cumin   **10 ml**
2 teaspoons cocoa   **10 ml**
1 teaspoon dried
   oregano   **5 ml**
Flour tortillas

- Cut sausage into ½-inch (1.2 cm) pieces.

- Combine all ingredients and 1 teaspoon (5 ml) salt except tortillas in slow cooker and stir well.

- Cover and cook on LOW for 5 to 7 hours.

- Serve with buttered, flour tortillas. Serves 6 to 8.

A Different Stew

2 pounds premium lean beef stew meat	910 g
1 (16 ounce) package frozen Oriental stir-fry vegetables, thawed	455 g
1 (10 ounce) can beefy mushroom soup	280 g
1 (10 ounce) can beef broth	280 g
⅔ cup bottled sweet-and-sour sauce	150 ml
1 tablespoon beef seasoning	15 ml

- Brown stew meat sprinkled with ½ teaspoon (2 ml) black pepper in skillet and place in slow cooker.

- Combine vegetables, soup, broth, sweet-and-sour sauce, beef seasoning and 1 cup (250 ml) water in bowl. Pour over stew meat and stir well.

- Cover and cook on LOW for 5 to 7 hours. Serves 4 to 6.

Chicken Stew

4 large boneless, skinless chicken breast halves, cubed	
3 medium potatoes, peeled, cubed	
1 (26 ounce) jar meatless spaghetti sauce	740 g
1 (15 ounce) can cut green beans, drained	425 g
1 (15 ounce) can whole kernel corn	425 g
1 tablespoon chicken seasoning	15 ml

- Combine chicken, potatoes, spaghetti sauce, green beans, corn, chicken seasoning and ¾ cup (175 ml) water in 5 to 6-quart (5 to 6 L) slow cooker.

- Cover and cook on LOW for 6 to 7 hours. Serves 4 to 6.

Southern Ham Stew

This is great served with cornbread.

2 cups dried black-eyed peas	480 g
3 cups cooked, cubed ham	420 g
1 large onion, chopped	
2 cups sliced celery	200 g
1 (15 ounce) can yellow hominy, drained	425 g
2 (15 ounce) cans stewed tomatoes	2 (425 g)
1 (10 ounce) can chicken broth	280 g
2 teaspoons seasoned salt	10 ml
2 tablespoons cornstarch	15 g

- Rinse and drain dried black-eyed peas in saucepan. Cover peas with water, bring to a boil and drain again.

- Place peas in large slow cooker and add 5 cups (1.2 L) water, ham, onion, celery, hominy, tomatoes, broth and seasoned salt.

- Cover and cook on LOW for 7 to 9 hours. Mix cornstarch with ⅓ cup (75 ml) water in bowl, turn cooker to HIGH heat, pour in cornstarch mixture and stir well.

- Cook for about 10 minutes or until stew thickens. Serves 6 to 8.

TIP: If you would like a little spice in the stew, substitute one of the cans of stewed tomatoes with the Mexican stewed tomatoes.

Serious Bean Stew

1 (16 ounce) package smoked sausage links	455 g
1 (28 ounce) can baked beans with liquid	795 g
1 (15 ounce) can great northern beans with liquid	425 g
1 (15 ounce) can pinto beans with liquid	425 g
1 (15 ounce) can lentil soup	425 g
1 onion, chopped	
1 teaspoon Cajun seasoning	5 ml
2 (15 ounce) cans stewed tomatoes	2 (425 g)
Corn muffins	

- Peel skin from sausage links and slice.

- Place in 6-quart (6 L) slow cooker, add remaining ingredients and stir to mix.

- Cover and cook on LOW for 3 to 4 hours.

- Serve with corn muffins. Serves 6 to 8.

Santa Fe Stew

A hearty, filling soup.

1½ pounds lean ground beef	680 g
1 (14 ounce) can beef broth	400 g
1 (15 ounce) can whole kernel corn with liquid	425 g
2 (15 ounce) cans pinto beans with liquid	2 (425 g)
2 (15 ounce) cans Mexican stewed tomatoes	2 (425 g)
1 teaspoon beef seasoning	4 ml
1 (16 ounce) package cubed Velveeta® cheese	455 g

- Brown beef in skillet until no longer pink.

- Place in 5 to 6-quart (5 to 6 L) slow cooker and add broth, corn, beans, tomatoes and beef seasoning.

- Cover and cook on LOW for 5 to 6 hours.

- When ready to serve, fold in cheese and stir until cheese melts. Serves 6 to 8.

TIP: Cornbread is a must to serve with this stew.

Pork-Vegetable Stew

1 (2 pound) pork
   tenderloin   910 g
1 onion, coarsely
   chopped
1 red bell pepper,
   julienned
1 (16 ounce) package
   frozen mixed
   vegetables, thawed   455 g
2 tablespoons flour   15 g
½ teaspoon dried
   rosemary leaves   2 ml
½ teaspoon oregano
   leaves   2 ml
1 (10 ounce) can chicken
   broth   280 g
1 (6 ounce) package
   long grain-wild rice   170 g

- Cut tenderloin into 1-inch (2.5 cm) cubes. Brown tenderloin cubes in non-stick skillet and place in large, sprayed slow cooker.

- Add onion, bell pepper and mixed vegetables.

- Combine flour, rosemary and oregano into chicken broth in bowl and pour over vegetables.

- Cover and cook on LOW for 4 hours to 4 hours 30 minutes.

- When ready to serve, cook rice according to package directions.

- Serve pork and vegetables over rice. Serves 4 to 6.

Roast and Vegetable Stew

3 cups leftover roast beef, cubed	420 g
2 (15 ounce) cans stewed tomatoes	2 (425 g)
1 (16 ounce) package frozen mixed vegetables, thawed	455 g
2 (14 ounce) cans beef broth	2 (400 g)
1 cup cauliflower florets	100 g
1 cup broccoli florets	70 g

- Combine all ingredients except cauliflower and broccoli in 6-quart (6 L) slow cooker. Add a little salt and pepper.

- Cover and cook on LOW for 3 to 4 hours.

- Stir in cauliflower and broccoli and continue cooking for an additional 2 hours until tender. Serves 6 to 8.

Olé! For Stew

1½ - 2 pounds lean beef stew meat	680 - 910 g
2 (15 ounce) cans pinto beans with liquid	2 (425 g)
1 onion, chopped	
3 carrots, sliced	
2 medium potatoes, cubed	
1 (1 ounce) packet taco seasoning	30 g
2 (15 ounce) cans Mexican stewed tomatoes	2 (425 g)
Flour tortillas	

- Brown stew meat in non-stick skillet. Combine meat, pinto beans, onion, carrots, potatoes, taco seasoning and 2 cups (500 ml) water in large slow cooker.

- Cover and cook on LOW for 6 to 7 hours. Add stewed tomatoes and cook for an additional 1 hour. Serves 4 to 6.

TIP: This is great served with warmed, buttered, flour tortillas.

Meatball Stew

1 (18 ounce) package frozen prepared Italian meatballs, thawed	510 g
1 (14 ounce) can beef broth	400 g
1 (15 ounce) can cut green beans	425 g
1 (16 ounce) package baby carrots	455 g
2 (15 ounce) cans stewed tomatoes	2 (425 g)
1 tablespoon Worcestershire sauce	15 ml
½ teaspoon ground allspice	2 ml

- Combine all ingredients in slow cooker.

- Cover and cook on LOW for 3 to 5 hours. Serves 4 to 6.

Meatball and Veggie Stew

1 (18 ounce) package frozen cooked meatballs, thawed	510 g
1 (16 ounce) package frozen mixed vegetables	455 g
1 (15 ounce) can stewed tomatoes	425 g
1 (12 ounce) jar beef gravy	340 g
2 teaspoons crushed dried basil	10 ml

- Place meatballs and mixed vegetables in 4 to 5-quart (4 to 5 L) slow cooker.

- Combine stewed tomatoes, gravy, basil, ½ teaspoon (2 ml) black pepper and ½ cup (125 ml) water in bowl. Pour over meatballs and vegetables.

- Cover and cook on LOW for 6 to 7 hours. Serves 4 to 6.

Italian-Vegetable Stew

1½ - 2 pounds Italian sausage	680 - 910 g
2 (16 ounce) packages frozen vegetables	2 (455 g)
2 (15 ounce) cans Italian stewed tomatoes	2 (425 g)
1 (14 ounce) can beef broth	400 g
1 teaspoon Italian seasoning	5 ml
½ cup pasta shells	55 g

- Brown sausage and cook in skillet for about 5 minutes and drain.

- Combine sausage, vegetables, stewed tomatoes, broth, Italian seasoning and shells in 5 to 6-quart (5 to 6 L) slow cooker and mix well.

- Cover and cook on LOW for 3 to 5 hours. Serves 4 to 6.

Hungarian Stew

2 pounds boneless short ribs	910 g
1 cup pearl barley	200 g
1 small onion, chopped	
1 green bell pepper, cored, seeded, chopped	
1 teaspoon minced garlic	5 ml
2 (15 ounce) cans kidney beans, drained	2 (425 g)
2 (14 ounce) cans beef broth	2 (400 g)
1 tablespoon paprika	15 ml

- Combine all ingredients plus 1 cup (250 ml) water in slow cooker.

- Cover and cook on LOW for 8 to 9 hours or on HIGH for 4 hours 30 minutes to 5 hours. Serves 4 to 6.

Hearty Meatball Stew

1 (28 ounce) package frozen meatballs, thawed	795 g
2 (15 ounce) cans Italian stewed tomatoes	2 (425 g)
2 (14 ounce) cans beef broth	2 (400 g)
2 (15 ounce) cans new potatoes	2 (425 g)
1 (16 ounce) package baby carrots	455 g
1 tablespoon Step 1 beef seasoning	15 ml
Corn muffins	

- Place meatballs, stewed tomatoes, beef broth, potatoes, carrots and beef seasoning in 6-quart (6 L) slow cooker.

- Cover and cook on LOW for 6 to 7 hours.

- Serve with corn muffins. Serves 6 to 8.

Ham and Cabbage Stew

2 (15 ounce) can Italian stewed tomatoes	2 (425 g)
3 cups shredded cabbage	210 g
1 onion, chopped	
1 red bell pepper, cored, seeded, chopped	
2 tablespoons butter, sliced	30 g
1 (14 ounce) can chicken broth	400 g
¾ teaspoon seasoned salt	4 ml
3 cups cooked, diced ham	420 g
Cornbread	

- Combine all ingredients with ¾ teaspoons (4 ml) pepper and 1 cup (250 ml) water in large slow cooker and stir to mix well.

- Cover and cook on LOW for 5 to 7 hours.

- Serve with cornbread. Serves 4 to 6.

South-of-the-Border Beef Stew

1½ - 2 pounds boneless, beef chuck roast	680 - 910 g
1 green bell pepper	
2 onions, coarsely chopped	
2 (15 ounce) cans pinto beans with liquid	2 (425 g)
½ cup rice	95 g
1 (14 ounce) can beef broth	400 g
2 (15 ounce) cans Mexican stewed tomatoes	2 (425 g)
1 cup mild or medium green salsa	265 g
2 teaspoons ground cumin	10 ml
Flour tortillas	

- Trim fat from beef and cut into 1-inch (2.5 cm) cubes.

- Brown beef in large skillet and place in large, sprayed slow cooker.

- Cut bell pepper into ½-inch (1.2 cm) slices.

- Add remaining ingredients plus 1½ cups (375 ml) water and a little salt.

- Cover and cook on LOW for 7 to 8 hours.

- Serve with warm, flour tortillas. Serves 6 to 8.

Comfort Stew

1½ pounds select stew meat	680 g
2 (10 ounce) cans French onion soup	2 (280 g)
1 (10 ounce) can cream of onion soup	280 g
1 (10 ounce) can cream of celery soup	280 g
1 (16 ounce) package frozen stew vegetables, thawed	455 g

- Place stew meat in sprayed slow cooker.

- Add soups as listed and spread evenly over meat. DO NOT STIR.

- Turn slow cooker to HIGH and cook just long enough for ingredients to get hot.

- Change heat setting to LOW, cover and cook for 6 to 7 hours. Add vegetables and continue cooking for additional 1 hour. Serves 4 to 6.

Chicken Stew over Biscuits

2 (1 ounce) packets chicken gravy mix	2 (30 g)
2 cups sliced celery	200 g
1 (10 ounce) package frozen sliced carrots	280 g
1 (10 ounce) package frozen green peas, thawed	280 g
1 teaspoon dried basil	5 ml
3 cups cubed cooked chicken	280 g
Buttermilk biscuits	

- Combine gravy mix, 2 cups (500 ml) water, celery, carrots, peas, basil, ¾ teaspoon (4 ml) each of salt and pepper and chicken in slow cooker.

- Cover and cook on LOW for 6 to 7 hours. Serve over baked refrigerated buttermilk biscuits. Serves 4 to 6.

TIP: *If you like thick stew, mix 2 tablespoons (15 g) cornstarch with ¼ cup (60 ml) water and stir into chicken mixture. Cook an additional 30 minutes to thicken.*

White Lightning Chili

3 (15 ounce) cans navy
  beans with
  liquid   3 (425 g)
3 (14 ounce) cans
  chicken broth   3 (400 g)
1 (10 ounce) can
  cream of chicken
  soup   280 g
2 tablespoons butter,
  melted   28 g
2 onions, chopped
3 cups cooked,
  chopped chicken
  or turkey   420 g
1 (7 ounce) can
  chopped green
  chilies   200 g

1 teaspoon minced
  garlic   5 ml
½ teaspoon dried
  basil   2 ml
½ teaspoon white
  pepper   2 ml
⅛ teaspoon cayenne
  pepper   .5 ml
⅛ teaspoon ground
  cloves   .5 ml
1 teaspoon ground
  oregano   5 ml
1 (8 ounce) package
  shredded 4-cheese
  blend   230 g

- Combine all ingredients except cheese in slow cooker.

- Cover and cook on LOW for 4 to 5 hours.

- When serving, sprinkle cheese over top of each serving. Serves 6 to 8.

Vegetarian Chili

2 (15 ounce) cans
   stewed tomatoes   2 (425 g)
1 (15 ounce) can
   kidney beans,
   rinsed, drained   425 g
1 (15 ounce) can pinto
   beans with liquid   425 g
1 onion, chopped
1 green bell pepper,
   seeded, chopped
1 tablespoon chili
   powder   15 ml
1 (7 ounce) package
   elbow macaroni   200 g
¼ cup (½ stick)
   butter, melted   60 g

- Combine tomatoes, kidney beans, pinto beans, onion, bell pepper, chili powder and 1 cup (250 ml) water in 4 to 5-quart (4 to 5 L) slow cooker.

- Cover and cook on LOW for 4 to 5 hours or on HIGH for 2 hours.

- Cook macaroni according to package directions, drain and stir in melted butter. Fold macaroni into chili.

- If desired, top each serving with shredded cheddar cheese. Serves 4 to 6.

Vegetable Chili

2 (15 ounce) cans navy
   beans with
    liquid   2 (425 g)
1 (15 ounce) can pinto
   beans with liquid   425 g
2 (15 ounce) cans
   Mexican stewed
    tomatoes   2 (425 g)
1 (15 ounce) can
   whole kernel corn 425 g
1 onion, chopped
3 ribs celery, sliced
1 tablespoon chili
   powder   15 ml
2 teaspoons dried
   oregano leaves   10 ml
1 teaspoon seasoned
   salt   5 ml
Broccoli cornbread

- In 5 to 6-quart (5 L) slow cooker, combine beans, tomatoes, corn, onion, celery, chili powder, oregano, seasoned salt and 1½ cups (375 ml) water.

- Cover and cook on LOW for 4 to 6 hours.

- Serve with hot, buttered broccoli cornbread. Serves 6 to 8.

Traditional Chili

2 pounds lean beef chili
    meat   910 g
1 large onion, finely
    chopped
1 (10 ounce) can chopped
    tomatoes and green
    chilies   280 g
2½ cups tomato juice   625 ml
2 tablespoons chili
    powder   15 g
1 tablespoon ground
    cumin   15 ml
1 tablespoon minced
    garlic   15 ml
1 (15 ounce) can pinto
    or kidney beans   425 g

- Combine chili meat, onion, tomatoes and green chilies, tomato juice, chili powder, cumin, garlic and 1 cup (250 ml) water in large slow cooker and mix well.

- Cover and cook on LOW for 7 to 9 hours.

- Add pinto or kidney beans and continue to cook for an additional 30 minutes. Serves 4 to 6.

Turkey-Veggie Chili

1 pound ground
    turkey   455 g
Canola oil
2 (15 ounce) cans
    pinto beans with
    liquid   2 (425 g)
1 (15 ounce) can great
    northern beans
    with liquid   425 g
1 (14 ounce) can
    chicken broth   400 g
2 (15 ounce) cans
Mexican stewed
    tomatoes   2 (425 g)
1 (8 ounce) can
    whole kernel corn 230 g
1 large onion,
    chopped
1 red bell pepper,
    chopped
2 teaspoons minced
    garlic   10 ml
2 teaspoons ground
    cumin   10 ml
½ cup elbow
    macaroni   55 g

- Cook and brown turkey in skillet with a little oil before placing in large slow cooker.

- Add beans, broth, tomatoes, corn, onion, bell pepper, garlic, cumin and a little salt and stir well.

- Cover and cook on LOW for 4 to 5 hours.

- Stir in macaroni and continue cooking for about 15 minutes. Stir to make sure macaroni does not stick to cooker and cook for an additional 15 minutes or until macaroni is tender. Serves 6 to 8.

TIP: Top each serving with dab of sour cream or 1 tablespoon (15 ml) shredded cheddar cheese.

Easy Chili

4 pounds lean ground beef	**1.8 kg**
2 (10 ounce) packages hot chili mix	**2 (280 g)**
1 (6 ounce) can tomato sauce	**170 g**
2 (15 ounce) cans stewed tomatoes with liquid	**425 g**
2½ teaspoons ground cumin	**12 ml**

- Break ground beef into pieces and brown in large skillet and drain. Use slotted spoon to drain fat and place beef in 5 to 6-quart (5 to 6 L) slow cooker.

- Add chili mix, tomato sauce, stewed tomatoes, cumin, 1 teaspoon (5 ml) salt and 1 cup (250 ml) water.

- Cover and cook on LOW for 4 to 5 hours. Serves 6 to 8.

TIP: If you think you can't eat chili without beans, add 2 (15 ounce/425 g) cans ranch-style beans.

Chunky Chili

2 pounds premium cut stew meat	910 g
1 onion, chopped	
2 (15 ounce) cans diced tomatoes	2 (425 g)
2 (15 ounce) cans pinto beans with liquid	2 (425 g)
1½ tablespoons chili powder	22 ml
2 teaspoons ground cumin	10 ml
1 teaspoon ground oregano	5 ml

- Shredded cheddar cheese

- If stew meat is in fairly large chunks, cut each chunk in half.

- Brown stew meat in large skillet and transfer to large slow cooker.

- Add onion, tomatoes, beans, chili powder, cumin, oregano and a little salt.

- Cover and cook on LOW for 6 to 7 hours.

- Sprinkle shredded cheddar cheese over each serving. Serves 4 to 6.

Ham-Vegetable Chowder

A great recipe for leftover ham.

1 medium potato	
1 cup diced ham	140 g
2 (10 ounce) cans cream of celery soup	2 (280 g)
1 (14 ounce) can chicken broth	400 g
3 cups finely diced ham	420 g
1 (15 ounce) can whole kernel corn	425 g
2 carrots, peeled, sliced	
1 onion, coarsely chopped	
1 teaspoon dried basil	5 ml
1 teaspoon seasoned salt	5 ml
1 (10 ounce) package frozen broccoli florets	280 g

- Cut potato into 1-inch (2.5 cm) pieces.

- Combine 1 teaspoon (5 ml) pepper and all ingredients except broccoli florets in large slow cooker.

- Cover and cook on LOW for 5 to 6 hours. Add broccoli to cooker and cook for an additional 1 hour. Serves 4 to 6.

TIP: If you don't like black specks in your chowder, use white pepper instead of black pepper.

Crab Chowder

2 small zucchini, thinly
    sliced
1 red bell pepper,
    julienned
2 ribs celery, diagonally
    sliced
1 medium potato,
    cubed
2 tablespoons butter,
    melted   30 g
1 (10 ounce) can
    chicken broth   280 g
1 teaspoon seasoned
    salt   5 ml
2 tablespoons
    cornstarch   15 g
3 cups milk   750 ml
2 (6 ounce) cans
    crabmeat,
    drained   2 (170 g)
1 (3 ounce) package
    cream cheese,
    cubed   85 g

- Place zucchini, bell pepper, celery, potato, butter, broth and seasoned salt in sprayed slow cooker.

- Stir cornstarch into milk in bowl; pour into slow cooker.

- Cover and cook on LOW for 3 to 4 hours.

- Turn heat to HIGH, add crabmeat and cream cheese and stir until cream cheese melts. Serves 4.

Country Chicken Chowder

1½ pounds boneless, skinless chicken breast halves	680 g
2 tablespoons butter	30 g
2 (10 ounce) cans cream of potato soup	2 (280 g)
1 (14 ounce) can chicken broth	400 g
1 (8 ounce) package frozen whole kernel corn	230 g
1 onion, sliced	
2 ribs celery, sliced	
1 (10 ounce) package frozen peas and carrots, thawed	280 g
½ teaspoon dried thyme leaves	2 ml
½ cup half-and-half cream	125 ml

- Cut chicken into 1-inch (2.5 cm) strips.

- Brown chicken strips in butter in skillet and transfer to large slow cooker.

- Add soup, broth, corn, onion, celery, peas and carrots, and thyme and stir.

- Cover and cook on LOW for 3 to 4 hours or until vegetables are tender.

- Turn off heat, stir in half-and-half cream and set aside for about 10 minutes before serving. Serves 4 to 6.

Chicken Chowder

3 cups cooked, cubed chicken	420 g
1 (14 ounce) can chicken broth	400 g
2 (10 ounce) cans cream of potato soup	2 (280 g)
1 large onion, chopped	
3 ribs celery, sliced diagonally	
1 (16 ounce) package frozen whole kernel corn, thawed	455 g
⅔ cup whipping cream	150 ml

- Combine chicken, chicken broth, potato soup, onion, celery, corn and ¾ cup (175 ml) water in 5 to 6-quart (5 to 6 L) slow cooker.

- Cover and cook on LOW for 3 to 4 hours.

- Add whipping cream to slow cooker and heat for additional 15 minutes or until thoroughly hot. Serves 4 to 6.

Oyster Chowder

1 small red bell pepper,
    seeded, chopped
1 onion, chopped
1 (14 ounce) can chicken
    broth   400 g
1 medium potato, cubed
1 fresh jalapeno pepper,
    seeded, finely chopped
8 ounces shucked oysters
    with liquid   230 g
1 (10 ounce) package
    frozen whole kernel
    corn, thawed   280 g
1 teaspoon dried oregano   5 ml
½ cup whipping cream   125 ml

- Combine all ingredients except
  cream in slow cooker.

- Cover and cook on LOW for
  3 to 4 hours.

- When ready to serve, stir in
  cream. Serves 4.

Split-Pea and Ham Chowder

1 medium potato
3 cups cooked, cubed
    ham   420 g
1 (16 ounce) bag split
    peas, rinsed   455 g
1 (11 ounce) can whole
    kernel corn with red
    and green peppers   310 g
1 (14 ounce) can chicken
    broth   400 g
2 carrots, sliced
2 ribs celery, diagonally
    sliced
1 tablespoon dried onion
    flakes   15 ml
1 teaspoon dried
    marjoram leaves   5 ml
1 teaspoon seasoned salt   5 ml

- Cut potato into small cubes and
  add to sprayed slow cooker.

- Add remaining ingredients plus
  3 cups (750 ml) water and
  1 teaspoon (5 ml) salt.

- Cover and cook on LOW for
  6 to 8 hours. Serves 4 to 6.

Corn-Ham Chowder

1 (14 ounce) can chicken broth	400 g
1 cup milk	250 ml
1 (10 ounce) can cream of celery soup	280 g
1 (15 ounce) can cream-style corn	425 g
1 (15 ounce) can whole kernel corn	425 g
½ cup dry potato flakes	30 g
1 onion, chopped	
2 - 3 cups cooked, chopped ham	280 - 420 g

- Combine broth, milk, soup, cream-style corn, whole kernel corn, potato flakes, onion and ham in 6-quart (6 L) slow cooker.

- Cover and cook on LOW for 4 to 5 hours.

- When ready to serve, season with a little salt and pepper. Serves 4 to 6.

Shrimp and Ham Jambalaya

3 ribs celery, diagonally
   slice
1 onion, chopped
1 red bell pepper,
   seeded, chopped
1 green bell pepper,
   seeded, chopped
2 (15 ounce) cans
   stewed tomatoes   2 (425 g)
2 cups cooked, cubed
   smoked ham   280 g
½ teaspoon cayenne
   pepper   2 ml
1 tablespoon dried
   parsley flakes   15 ml
2 teaspoons minced
   garlic   30 ml
1 pound peeled,
   veined shrimp   455 g
Rice, cooked

- Combine celery, onion, bell peppers, tomatoes, ham, cayenne pepper, parsley flakes, garlic and a little salt and pepper in sprayed slow cooker.

- Cover and cook on LOW for 7 to 8 hours or on HIGH for 3 to 4 hours.

- Stir in shrimp and cook on LOW for 1 hour.

- Serve over rice. Serves 4 to 6.

Shrimp and Sausage Jambalaya

1 pound cooked, smoked sausage links	455 g
1 onion, chopped	
1 green bell pepper, chopped	
2 teaspoons minced garlic	10 ml
1 (28 ounce) can diced tomatoes	795 g
1 tablespoon parsley flakes	15 ml
½ teaspoon dried thyme leaves	2 ml
1 teaspoon Cajun seasoning	5 ml
¼ teaspoon cayenne pepper	1 ml
1 pound peeled, veined shrimp	455 g
Rice, cooked	

- Combine all ingredients except shrimp and rice in sprayed slow cooker.

- Cover and cook on LOW for 6 to 8 hours or on HIGH for 3 to 4 hours.

- Stir in shrimp and cook on LOW for an additional 1 hour. Serve over rice. Serves 4 to 6.

Shrimp and Chicken Jambalaya

4 chicken breast halves,
   cubed
1 (28 ounce) can diced
   tomatoes   795 g
1 onion, chopped
1 green bell pepper,
   seeded, chopped
1 (14 ounce) can chicken
   broth   400 g
½ cup dry white wine
   or cooking wine   125 ml
2 teaspoons dried
   oregano   10 ml
2 teaspoons Cajun
   seasoning   10 ml
½ teaspoon cayenne
   pepper   2 ml
1 pound cooked, peeled,
   veined shrimp   455 g
2 cups cooked white rice   370 g

- Place all ingredients except shrimp and rice in slow cooker and stir.

- Cover and cook on LOW for 6 to 8 hours.

- Turn heat to HIGH, stir in shrimp and rice and cook for an additional 15 to 20 minutes. Serves 4 to 6.

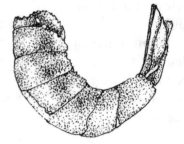

Veggies & Side Dishes

Baked, Braised, Crunched & Stewed

Veggies & Side Dishes Contents

Broccoli-Cheese Bake. 99
Savory Broccoli and Cauliflower 99
Broccoli and Cheese 100
Company Broccoli 101
Sunshine Green Beans. 101
Green Beans to Enjoy 103
Green Bean Revenge. 104
Crunchy Green Beans 105
Cajun Beans and Rice 105
A Different Bean. 106
Beans and More Beans 106
Better Butter Beans. 107
Italian Beans. 107
Creamy Limas. 108
Chili Frijoles. 109
Cinnamon Carrots. 110
Krazy Karrots 111
Squash Combo 111
Sunny Yellow Squash 112
Golden Squash 113
Super Corn .114
Yummy Corn. 114
Creamed Peas and Potatoes. 115
Creamed Cheese Spinach 115
Cheese-Please Spinach 116

Healthy Veggies 117
Harvest-Vegetable Casserole. 117
Golden Veggies. 118
Four Veggie Bake 118
California Vegetables 119
Creamed New Potatoes 120
Pretty Parsley Potatoes 120
Potatoes al Grande 121
Roasted New Potatoes. 122
Good Old Cheesy Potatoes 123
Glory Potatoes 124
Easy Baked Potatoes. 124
Dressed-Up Hash Browns 125
Company Potatoes 126
Cheezy Potatoes 126
Sweet Potatoes and Pineapple 127
Cheesy Ranch Potatoes 128
Glazed Sweet Potatoes 128
Hoppin' John. 129
Spicy Spanish Rice 129
Delicious Risotto Rice 130
Crunchy Couscous 130
Carnival Couscous 131
St. Pat's Noodles. 131
Cheese-Spaghetti and Spinach 132

Broccoli-Cheese Bake

¼ cup (½ stick) butter, melted	55 g
1 (10 ounce) can cream of mushroom soup	280 g
1 (10 ounce) can cream of onion soup	280 g
1 cup instant rice	95 g
1 (8 ounce) package cubed Velveeta® cheese	230 g
2 (10 ounce) packages frozen chopped broccoli, thawed	2 (280 g)

- Combine all ingredients, plus ½ cup (125 ml) water in sprayed slow cooker and stir well.

- Cover and cook on HIGH for 2 to 3 hours. Serves 4 to 6.

Savory Broccoli and Cauliflower

1 (16 ounce) package frozen broccoli florets, thawed	455 g
1 (16 ounce) package frozen cauliflower florets, thawed	455 g
2 (10 ounce) cans nacho cheese soup	2 (280 g)
6 slices bacon, cooked, crumbled	

- Place broccoli and cauliflower in sprayed slow cooker. Sprinkle with a little salt and pepper.

- Spoon soup over top and sprinkle with bacon. Cover and cook on LOW for 3 to 4 hours. Serves 6 to 8.

Broccoli and Cheese

2 (16 ounce) packages
   frozen broccoli
   florets, thawed   2 (425 g)
2 (15 ounce) cans
   whole new
   potatoes, drained   2 (425 g)
2 (10 ounce) cans
   cream of celery
   soup   2 (280 g)
½ cup milk   125 ml
1 (8 ounce) package
   shredded cheddar
   cheese, divided   230 g
1½ cups cracker
   crumbs, divided   90 g

- Place broccoli on plate, cut off stems and discard. Combine broccoli and potatoes in slow cooker.

- Combine soup and milk in saucepan, heat just enough to mix well and pour over broccoli and potatoes.

- Sprinkle half cheese and crumbs over broccoli.

- Cover and cook on LOW for 3 to 4 hours.

- When ready to serve, sprinkle remaining cheese and crumbs over top. Serves 6 to 8.

Company Broccoli

1½ pounds fresh broccoli, trimmed well	680 g
1 (10 ounce) can cream of chicken soup	280 g
½ cup mayonnaise	110 g
1 (8 ounce) package shredded cheddar cheese, divided	230 g
¼ cup toasted slivered almonds	40 g

- Place broccoli in sprayed slow cooker.

- Combine chicken soup, mayonnaise, half cheese and ¼ cup (60 ml) water in bowl. Spoon over broccoli.

- Cover and cook on LOW for 2 to 3 hours. When ready to serve, sprinkle remaining cheese over broccoli and top with toasted almonds. Serves 6 to 8.

Sunshine Green Beans

2 (16 ounce) packages frozen whole green beans, thawed	2 (455 g)
2 (10 ounce) cans fiesta nacho cheese soup	2 (280 g)
1 (8 ounce) package seasoning blend onions and bell peppers	230 g
1 (8 ounce) can sliced water chestnuts, cut in half	230 g
1 teaspoon seasoned salt	5 ml

- Combine all ingredients plus ¼ cup (60 ml) water in large slow cooker and stir to mix well.

- Cover and cook on LOW for 4 to 5 hours. Serves 6 to 8.

Southern Green Beans and Potatoes

6 - 8 medium new potatoes
    with peels, sliced
5 cups fresh whole green
    beans, trimmed   **355 g**
2 tablespoons dry,
    minced onions   **30 ml**
¼ cup (½ stick) butter,
    melted   **60 g**
1 (10 ounce) can cream
    of celery soup   **280 g**
1 (10 ounce) can fiesta
    nacho cheese soup **280 g**

- Place potatoes, green beans and minced onions in sprayed slow cooker.

- Pour melted butter over vegetables.

- Combine soups and ⅓ cup (75 ml) water in saucepan. Heat just enough to be able to mix soups and pour over vegetables.

- Cover and cook on LOW for 7 to 8 hours. Serves 6 to 8.

Green Beans to Enjoy

**2 pounds fresh green
    beans   910 g**
1 onion, finely chopped
4 thick slices bacon
**5 - 6 medium new (red)
    potatoes**
1 teaspoon sugar   5 ml

- Snap and wash green beans, place beans and onion in sprayed 5 to 6-quart (5 to 6 L) slow cooker.

- Cut bacon in 1-inch (2.5 cm) pieces and fry in skillet until crisp.

- Remove some of deeper "eyes" in new potatoes and cut into quarters.

- Add cooked bacon pieces, potatoes and 1 cup (250 ml) water to slow cooker.

- Add about 1 teaspoon (5 ml) each of salt and sugar. (A touch of sugar always helps fresh vegetables.)

- Cover and cook on LOW for 3 to 4 hours. Serves 6 to 8.

Green Bean Revenge

2 (16 ounce) packages
  frozen whole green
  beans, thawed   2 (425 g)
2 (8 ounce) cans sliced
  water chestnuts,
  drained   2 (230 g)
1 (16 ounce) package
  cubed jalapeno
  Velveeta® cheese   455 g
1 (10 ounce) can
  tomatoes and
  green chilies   280 g
¼ cup (½ stick)
  butter, melted   55 g
1 tablespoon chicken
  seasoning   15 ml
1½ cups slightly
  crushed potato
  chips   85 g

- Combine green beans, water chestnuts, cheese, tomatoes and green chilies, melted butter and seasoning in slow cooker and mix well.

- Cover and cook on LOW for 3 to 5 hours. Just before serving, cover top with crushed potato chips. Serves 6 to 8.

TIP: If you would like this to be a one-dish meal, add 2 to 3 cups (280 to 420 g) cooked, cubed ham.

Crunchy Green Beans

2 (16 ounce) packages
   frozen whole green
   beans, thawed   2 (455 g)
3 ribs celery,
   diagonally sliced
1 red bell pepper,
   julienned
2 (11 ounce) cans
   sliced water
   chestnuts, drained 2 (310 g)
1 (10 ounce) can
   cream of chicken
   soup   280 g
½ cup slivered
   almonds   85 g
1 (3 ounce) can
   french-fried
   onion rings   85 g

- Combine green beans, celery, bell pepper, water chestnuts, chicken soup and almonds in sprayed slow cooker.

- Cover and cook on LOW for 2 to 4 hours. About 10 minutes before serving, top with fried onion rings. Serves 6 to 8.

Cajun Beans and Rice

1 pound dry black or
   kidney beans   455 g
2 onions, chopped
2 teaspoons minced
   garlic   10 ml
1 tablespoon ground
   cumin   15 ml
1 (14 ounce) can
   chicken broth   400 g
1 cup instant brown
   rice   95 g

- Place beans in saucepan, cover with water and soak overnight.

- Combine beans, onion, garlic, cumin, chicken broth, 2 teaspoons (10 ml) salt and 2 cups (500 ml) water to 4 to 5-quart (4 to 5 L) slow cooker.

- Cover and cook on LOW for 4 to 6 hours.

A Different Bean

3 (15 ounce) cans
   black beans,
   rinsed, drained   3 (425 g)
3 (15 ounce) cans
   great northern
   beans, rinsed,
   drained   3 (425 g)
1 (16 ounce) jar hot,
   thick-and-chunky
   salsa   455 g
½ cup packed brown
   sugar   110 g

- Combine black beans, northern beans, salsa and brown sugar in 5 to 6-quart (5 to 6 L) slow cooker.

- Cover and cook on LOW for 3 to 4 hours. Serves 6 to 8.

TIP: To include pinto beans in this dish, use only 2 cans black beans and 1 can pinto beans.

Beans and More Beans

4 thick slices bacon,
   cooked crisp,
   crumbled
1 (15 ounce) can kidney
   beans, drained   425 g
1 (15 ounce) can lima
   beans with liquid   425 g
1 (15 ounce) can pinto
   beans with liquid   425 g
1 (15 ounce) can navy
   beans with liquid   425 g
1 (15 ounce) can pork
   and beans with liquid 425 g
1 onion, chopped
¾ cup chili sauce   205 g
1 cup packed brown
   sugar   220 g
1 tablespoon
   Worcestershire sauce 15 ml

- Combine all ingredients in sprayed slow cooker and mix well.

- Cover and cook on LOW for 5 to 6 hours. Serves 6 to 8.

Better Butter Beans

2 cups sliced celery	200 g
2 onions, chopped	
1 green bell pepper, julienned	
1 (15 ounce) can stewed tomatoes	425 g
¼ cup (½ stick) butter, melted	60 g
1 tablespoon chicken seasoning	15 ml
3 (15 ounce) cans butter beans, drained	3 (425 g)

- Combine all ingredients in slow cooker and mix well.

- Cover and cook on LOW for 3 to 4 hours. Serves 6 to 8.

TIP: You can make this a one-dish dinner, add 2 to 3 cups (280 to 420 g) cooked, cubed ham.

Italian Beans

2 (15 ounce) cans garbanzo beans, drained	2 (425 g)
1 (15 ounce) can red kidney beans, drained	425 g
1 (15 ounce) can cannellini beans, drained	425 g
2 (15 ounce) cans great northern beans, drained	2 (425 g)
1 teaspoon Italian seasoning	5 ml
1 (1 ounce) packet dry onion soup mix	30 g
1 teaspoon minced garlic	5 ml
½ cup beef broth	125 ml

- Combine all ingredients in slow cooker and stir well.

- Cover and cook on LOW for 5 to 6 hours or on HIGH for 2 hours 30 minutes to 3 hours. Serves 6 to 8.

Creamy Limas

2 (16 ounce) packages
   frozen baby lima
   beans, thawed   2 (455 g)
1 (10 ounce) can
   cream of celery   280 g
1 (10 ounce) can
   cream of onion
   soup   280 g
1 red bell pepper,
   cored, seeded,
   julienned
1 (4 ounce) jar sliced
   mushrooms,
   drained   115 g
¼ cup milk   60 ml
1 cup shredded
   cheddar-colby
   cheese   115 g

- Combine lima beans, soups, bell pepper, mushrooms and ½ teaspoon (2 ml) salt in saucepan and heat just enough to mix well.

- Pour into sprayed 4 to 5-quart (4 to 5 L) slow cooker. Stir well.

- Cover and cook on LOW for 8 to 9 hours.

- Just before serving, stir in milk. Spoon limas to serving bowl and sprinkle cheese over top. Serves 6 to 8.

Chili Frijoles

2 cups dry pinto beans	525 g
2 onions, finely chopped	
2 tablespoons chili powder	30 ml
1 teaspoon minced garlic	5 ml
1 (15 ounce) can tomato sauce	425 g
1½ pounds lean ground beef	680 g

- Soak beans overnight in water. Drain and transfer beans to large slow cooker. Add onion, chili powder, garlic, tomato sauce and 8 cups (1.9 L) water.

- Brown ground beef in skillet, drain and transfer to cooker.

- Cover and cook on LOW for 8 to 9 hours or until beans are tender and stir occasionally. Stir in 1 teaspoon (5 ml) salt just before serving. Serves 6 to 8.

TIP: If you forget to soak beans overnight, here's Plan B. Place beans in large saucepan and cover with water. Bring to a boil, turn off heat and let stand for 1 hour.

Cinnamon Carrots

2 (16 ounce) packages
    baby carrots   2 (455 g)
¾ cup packed brown
    sugar   165 g
¼ cup honey   85 g
½ cup orange juice   125 ml
2 tablespoons butter,
    melted   30 g
¾ teaspoon ground
    cinnamon   4 ml

- Place carrots in sprayed 3 to 4-quart (3 to 4 L) slow cooker.

- Combine brown sugar, honey, orange juice, butter and cinnamon in bowl and mix well. Pour over carrots and mix so sugar-cinnamon mixture coats carrots.

- Cover and cook on LOW for 3 hours 30 minutes to 4 hours and stir twice during cooking time.

- About 20 minutes before serving, transfer carrots with slotted spoon to serving dish and cover to keep warm.

- Pour liquid from cooker into saucepan; boil for several minutes until liquid reduces by half. Spoon over carrots in serving dish. Serves 6 to 8.

Krazy Karrots

1 (16 ounce) package baby carrots	455 g
¼ cup (½ stick) butter, melted	60 g
⅔ cup packed brown sugar	150 g
1 (1 ounce) packet ranch dressing mix	30g

- Combine carrots, melted butter, brown sugar, ranch dressing mix and ¼ cup (60 ml) water in 4-quart (4 L) slow cooker and stir well.

- Cover and cook on LOW for 3 to 4 hours and stir occasionally. Serves 4.

Squash Combo

1½ pounds small yellow squash	680 g
1½ pounds zucchini	680 g
1 teaspoon seasoned salt	5 ml
¼ cup (½ stick) butter, melted	60 g
½ cup seasoned breadcrumbs	60 g
½ cup shredded cheddar cheese	60 g

- Cut both yellow squash and zucchini in small pieces.

- Place in sprayed slow cooker and sprinkle with seasoned salt and pepper.

- Pour melted butter over squash and sprinkle with breadcrumbs and cheese.

- Cover and cook on LOW for 5 to 6 hours. Serves 6 to 8.

Sunny Yellow Squash

2 pounds medium yellow squash, sliced	910 g
2 onions, coarsely chopped	
3 ribs celery, diagonally sliced	
1 green bell pepper, cored, seeded, julienned	
1 (8 ounce) package cream cheese, cubed	230 g
1 teaspoon sugar	5 ml
¼ cup (½ stick) butter, melted	60 g
1 (10 ounce) can cheddar cheese soup	280 g
1½ cups crushed croutons	180 g

- Combine all ingredients, except breadcrumbs in slow cooker and mix well. Add 1 teaspoon (5 ml) each of salt and pepper.

- Cover and cook on LOW for 3 to 4 hours. Before serving, sprinkle top with breadcrumbs. Serves 6 to 8.

TIP: If you don't like black specks, use white pepper instead of black pepper.

Golden Squash

1 pound yellow squash,
    thinly sliced   455 g
1 pound zucchini, thinly
    sliced   455 g
3 ribs celery, sliced
1 onion, chopped
1 (10 ounce) can cream
    of chicken soup   280 g
1 (8 ounce) carton sour
    cream   230 g
3 tablespoons flour   20 g
1 (6 ounce) package
    seasoned stuffing
    mix   170 g
½ cup (1 stick) butter,
    melted   115 g

- Combine squash, zucchini, celery, onion and soup in large bowl.

- In separate bowl, mix sour cream with flour and stir into vegetables.

- Toss stuffing with melted butter in bowl and spoon half into slow cooker.

- Top with vegetables and spoon remaining stuffing on top.

- Cover and cook on LOW for 5 to 7 hours. Serves 6 to 8.

Super Corn

2 (15 ounce) cans
   whole kernel
   corn   **2 (425 g)**
2 (15 ounce) cans
   creamed corn   **2 (425 g)**
½ cup (1 stick) butter,
   melted   **115 g**
1 (8 ounce) carton
   sour cream   **230 g**
1 (8 ounce) package
   jalapeno
   cornbread mix   **230 g**

- Combine all ingredients in large bowl and mix well.

- Pour into sprayed slow cooker, cover and cook on LOW for 4 to 5 hours. Serves 6 to 8.

TIP: Make this a one-dish meal by adding 2 to 3 cups (280 to 420 g) leftover, cubed ham.

Yummy Corn

1 (8 ounce) and
   1 (3 ounce)
   package cream
   cheese   **230 g/85 g**
½ cup (1 stick)
   butter, melted **115 g**
2 (16 ounce) packages
   frozen whole
   kernel corn,
   thawed   **2 (455 g)**

- Turn sprayed 4-quart (4 L) slow cooker to HIGH and add cream cheese and butter.

- Cook just until cheese and butter melt and stir. Add corn and a little salt and pepper.

- Cover and cook on LOW for 1 hour 30 minutes to 2 hours. Serves 4 to 6.

Creamed Peas and Potatoes

2 pounds small (red)
  new potatoes with
  peels, quartered   910 g
1 (16 ounce) package
  frozen green peas
  with pearl onions,
  thawed   455 g
2 (10 ounce) cans
  fiesta nacho
  cheese soup   2 (280 g)
½ cup milk   125 ml

- Sprinkle potatoes with a little salt and pepper, place in sprayed slow cooker and place peas on top.

- Combine nacho cheese soup and milk in saucepan, heat just enough to mix well and spoon over peas.

- Cover and cook on LOW for 4 to 5 hours. Serves 6 to 8.

Creamed Cheese Spinach

2 (10 ounce) packages
  frozen chopped
  spinach   2 (280 g)
1 (16 ounce) carton
  small curd cottage
  cheese   455 g
1½ cups shredded
  American or
  cheddar cheese   170 g
3 eggs, beaten
¼ cup (½ stick)
  butter, melted   60 g
¼ cup flour   30 g

- Squeeze spinach between paper towels to completely remove excess moisture.

- Combine all ingredients in bowl and mix well. Spoon into sprayed slow cooker.

- Cover and cook on HIGH for 1 hour, change heat to LOW and cook for an additional 3 to 5 hours or until knife inserted in center comes out clean. Serves 4 to 6.

Cheese-Please Spinach

1 (10 ounce) and
   1 (16 ounce) package
   chopped spinach,
   thawed, drained   280 g/455 g
1 (8 ounce) package
   cream cheese,
   cubed, softened   230 g
1 (10 ounce) can
   cream of chicken
   soup   280 g
1 egg, beaten
1 (8 ounce) package
   shredded cheddar
   cheese   230 g

- Squeeze spinach between paper towels to completely remove excess moisture.

- Combine spinach, cream cheese, chicken soup, egg and a little salt and pepper in large bowl. Spoon into sprayed slow cooker.

- Cover and cook on LOW for 3 to 4 hours.

- Before serving, stir in cheddar cheese. Serves 4 to 6.

Healthy Veggies

1 (16 ounce) package frozen broccoli, cauliflower and carrots	455 g
2 medium zucchini, halved lengthwise, sliced	
1 (1 ounce) packet ranch dressing mix	30 g
2 tablespoons butter, melted	30 g

- Place broccoli, cauliflower and carrots, and zucchini in 4-quart (4 L) slow cooker.

- Combine ranch dressing mix, melted butter and ½ cup (125 ml) water in bowl, spoon over vegetables and stir.

- Cover and cook on LOW for 2 to 3 hours. Serves 4.

Harvest-Vegetable Casserole

3 - 4 medium new (red) potatoes with peels, sliced	
2 onions, sliced	
3 carrots, sliced	
2 cups chopped green cabbage	140 g
¼ cup Italian dressing	60 ml
1 (1 pound) kielbasa sausage	455 g
1 (15 ounce) can Italian stewed tomatoes	425 g

- Place potatoes, onions, carrots, cabbage and Italian dressing in large, sprayed slow cooker.

- Cut sausage into 1-inch (2.5 cm) pieces and place on top of vegetables.

- Drizzle stewed tomatoes in even layers over vegetables.

- Cover and cook on LOW for 6 to 8 hours or until vegetables are tender. Serves 4 to 6.

Golden Veggies

1 (16 ounce) package
   frozen cauliflower
   florets, thawed   455 g
1 (15 ounce) can whole
   kernel corn   425 g
¾ pound small yellow
   squash, chopped   340 g
¼ cup (½ stick) butter,
   melted   60 g
2 (10 ounce) cans
   cheddar cheese
   soup   2 (280 g)
6 slices bacon,
   cooked, crumbled

- Place cauliflower, corn and squash in sprayed slow cooker and sprinkle with a little salt and pepper.

- Pour melted butter over vegetables and spoon cheese soup on top. Sprinkle with crumbled bacon.

- Cover and cook on LOW for 4 to 5 hours. Serves 4 to 6.

Four Veggie Bake

1 (10 ounce) package
   frozen broccoli
   florets, thawed   280 g
1 (10 ounce) package
   frozen cauliflower,
   thawed   280 g
1 (10 ounce) package
   frozen brussels
   sprouts   280 g
4 small yellow squash,
   sliced
1 (10 ounce) can cream of
   mushroom soup   280 g
1 (16 ounce) package
   cubed Velveeta®
   cheese   455 g

- Place vegetables in sprayed slow cooker.

- Layer soup and cheese on top of vegetables.

- Cover and cook on LOW for 3 to 4 hours. Serves 4 to 6.

California Vegetables

1 (16 ounce) package frozen vegetable mix, thawed	455 g
1 (10 ounce) package frozen green peas, thawed	280 g
1 (10 ounce) package frozen whole kernel corn, thawed	280 g
2 (10 ounce) cans cream of mushroom soup	2 (280 g)
1 cup instant white rice	95 g
1 (8 ounce) package cubed Velveeta® cheese	230 g
1 cup milk	250 ml
2 tablespoons butter, melted	30 g
1 teaspoon seasoned salt	5 ml

- Place all vegetables in large, sprayed slow cooker.

- Combine soup, rice, cheese, milk, butter, seasoned salt and 1 cup (250 ml) water in saucepan, heat just enough to mix and pour over vegetables.

- Cover and cook on LOW for 4 to 5 hours. Stir before serving. Serves 6 to 8.

Creamed
New Potatoes

2 - 2½ pounds new (red) potatoes with peels, quartered	910 g
1 (8 ounce) package cream cheese, softened	230 g
1 (10 ounce) can fiesta nacho soup	280 g
1 (1 ounce) packet buttermilk ranch salad dressing mix	30 g
1 cup milk	250 ml

- Place potatoes in 6-quart (6 L) slow cooker.

- Beat cream cheese until creamy and fold in fiesta nacho soup, ranch salad dressing mix and milk. Stir into potatoes.

- Cover and cook on LOW for 3 to 4 hours or until potatoes are well done. Serves 4 to 6.

Pretty Parsley
Potatoes

2 pounds new (red) potatoes with peels, quartered	910 g
¼ cup canola oil	60 ml
1 (0.4 ounce) packet ranch dressing mix	10 g
¼ cup chopped fresh parsley	15 g

- Place potatoes, oil, dressing mix and ¼ cup (60 ml) water in 4 to 5-quart (4 to 5 L) slow cooker and toss to coat potatoes.

- Cover and cook on LOW for 3 to 4 hours or until potatoes are tender.

- When ready to serve, sprinkle parsley over potatoes and toss. Serves 4 to 6.

Potatoes al Grande

6 medium potatoes,
   peeled
1 (8 ounce) package
   shredded cheddar
   cheese, divided   230 g
1 (10 ounce) can cream
   of chicken soup   280 g
¼ cup (½ stick) butter,
   melted   60 g
1 (8 ounce) carton sour
   cream   230 g
1 (3 ounce) can
   french-fried onion
   rings   85 g

- Cut potatoes in 1-inch (2.5 cm) strips. Toss potatoes with a little salt and pepper plus 2 cups (230 g) cheese. Place in slow cooker.

- Combine soup, melted butter and 2 tablespoons (30 ml) water in saucepan and heat just enough to pour over potato mixture.

- Cover and cook on LOW for 6 to 8 hours or until potatoes are tender.

- Stir in sour cream and remaining cheese.

- When ready to serve, sprinkle onion rings over top of potatoes. Serves 4 to 6.

Roasted New Potatoes

18 - 20 new (red) potatoes
    with peels
¼ cup (½ stick) butter,
    melted   **60 g**
1 tablespoon dried
    parsley   **15 ml**
½ teaspoon garlic powder **2 ml**
½ teaspoon paprika   **2 ml**

- Combine all ingredients plus ½ teaspoon (2 ml) each of salt and pepper in sprayed slow cooker and mix well.

- Cover and cook on LOW for 7 hours or on HIGH for 3 hours 30 minutes to 4 hours.

- When ready to serve, remove potatoes with slotted spoon to serving dish and cover to keep warm.

- Add about 2 tablespoons (30 ml) water to drippings and stir until they blend well.

- Pour mixture over potatoes. Serves 4 to 6.

Good Old Cheesy Potatoes

1 (28 ounce) package frozen hash-brown potatoes with onions and peppers, thawed	795 g
2 (10 ounce) cans cream of chicken soup	2 (280 g)
1 (8 ounce) carton sour cream	230 g
½ cup (1 stick) butter, melted, divided	115 g
1 (8 ounce) package shredded cheddar cheese	230 g
2 tablespoons dried parsley	30 ml
2 cups dry stuffing mix	120 g

- Combine potatoes, soup, sour cream, ¼ cup (57 g) melted butter, cheese, parsley and 1 teaspoon (5 ml) salt in large bowl and mix well.

- Spoon mixture into large slow cooker. Sprinkle stuffing mix over potato mixture and drizzle remaining butter over stuffing.

- Cover and cook on LOW for 7 to 9 hours or on HIGH for 3 to 4 hours. Serves 4 to 6.

Glory Potatoes

1 (10 ounce) can cream of
  chicken soup   280 g
1 (8 ounce) carton sour
  cream   230 g
2 pounds potatoes,
  peeled, cubed   910 g
1 (8 ounce) package
  shredded cheddar
  Jack cheese   230 g
1 cup crushed potato
  chips   55 g

- Combine soup, sour cream,
  ¼ cup (60 ml) water and a little
  salt and pepper in bowl.

- Combine potatoes and cheese
  in 5-quart (5 L) slow cooker.
  Spoon soup-sour cream mixture
  over potatoes.

- Cover and cook on LOW for
  8 to 9 hours.

- When ready to serve, sprinkle
  crushed potato chips over
  potatoes. Serves 4 to 6.

Easy Baked Potatoes

6 medium russet potatoes
  with peels
¼ - ½ cup canola oil   60 - 125 ml
Butter
Sour cream

- Pierce potatoes with fork.
  Brush potato skins with oil and
  sprinkle a little salt and pepper
  on potato skins.

- Wrap potatoes individually in
  foil and place in large
  slow cooker.

- Cover and cook on LOW for
  7 to 8 hours or until potatoes
  are tender.

- Prepare assorted toppings such
  as: shredded cheese, salsa, ranch
  dip, chopped green onions,
  bacon bits, chopped boiled eggs,
  cheese-hamburger dip, broccoli-
  cheese soup, etc. Serves 6.

Dressed-Up Hash Browns

1 (26 ounce) package
    frozen hash-brown
    potatoes with onions
    and peppers   740 g
Canola oil
2 - 3 cups chopped
    cooked ham   280 - 420 g
1 (16 ounce) carton
    sour cream   455 g
1 (8 ounce) package
    shredded cheddar
    Jack cheese   230 g
1 (3 ounce) can
    french-fried
    onion rings   85 g

- Cook potatoes in a little oil in large skillet. Transfer to 5 to 6-quart (5 to 6 L) slow cooker.

- Combine ham, sour cream and cheese in bowl and mix into hash browns.

- Cover and cook on LOW for 2 to 3 hours.

- Dress potatoes up by sprinkling onion rings on top of cheese. Serves 4 to 6.

Company Potatoes

1 (5 ounce) box scalloped potatoes	145 g
1 (5 ounce) box au gratin potatoes	145 g
1 cup milk	250 ml
6 tablespoons (¾ stick) butter, melted	85 g
½ pound bacon, cooked crisp, crumbled	230 g

- Place both boxes of potatoes in sprayed slow cooker. Combine milk, butter and 4¼ cups (1.1 L) water in bowl and pour over potatoes.

- Cover and cook on LOW for 4 to 5 hours.

- When ready to serve, sprinkle crumbled bacon over top of potatoes. Serves 4 to 6.

Cheezy Potatoes

1 (28 ounce) bag frozen diced potatoes with onions and peppers, thawed	795 g
1 (8 ounce) package shredded Monterey Jack and cheddar cheese blend	230 g
1 (10 ounce) can cream of celery soup	280 g
1 (8 ounce) carton sour cream	230 g

- Combine potatoes, cheese, soup, sour cream and 1 teaspoon (5 ml) pepper in sprayed 5 to 6-quart (5 to 6 L) slow cooker and mix well.

- Cover and cook on LOW 4 to 6 hours. Stir well before serving. Serves 6 to 8.

Sweet Potatoes and Pineapple

3 (15 ounce) cans
  sweet potatoes,
  drained   3 (425 g)
½ (20 ounce) can
  pineapple pie
  filling   ½ (570 g)
2 tablespoons butter,
  melted   30 g
½ cup packed brown
  sugar   110 g
½ teaspoon ground
  cinnamon   2 ml

- Place sweet potatoes, pie filling, melted butter, brown sugar and cinnamon in sprayed 4 to 5-quart (4 L) slow cooker and lightly stir.

- Cover and cook on LOW for 2 to 3 hours. Serves 6 to 8.

Topping:

1 cup packed light
  brown sugar   220 g
3 tablespoons butter,
  melted   40 g
½ cup flour   60 g
1 cup coarsely chopped
  nuts   110 g

- While potatoes cook, combine topping ingredients in bowl, spread out on foil-lined baking pan and bake at 350° (175° C) for 15 to 20 minutes.

- When ready to serve, sprinkle topping over sweet potatoes.

Cheesy Ranch Potatoes

2½ pounds new (red)
  potatoes with peels,
  quartered   910 g
1 onion, cut into 8 wedges
1 (10 ounce) can fiesta
  nacho cheese soup   280 g
1 (8 ounce) carton sour
  cream   230 g
1 (1 ounce) packet ranch
  salad dressing mix   30 g
Chopped fresh parsley,
  optional

- Place potatoes and onion in sprayed 4 to 5-quart (4 to 5 L) slow cooker.

- Combine, nacho cheese soup, sour cream and dressing mix in bowl and whisk well to mix. Spoon over potato-onion mixture.

- Cover and cook on LOW for 6 to 7 hours.

- To serve, sprinkle chopped fresh parsley over potato mixture. Serves 4 to 6.

Glazed Sweet Potatoes

3 (15 ounce) cans
  sweet potatoes,
  drained   3 (425 g)
¼ cup (½ stick)
  butter, melted   60 g
2 cups packed
  brown sugar   440 g
⅓ cup orange juice   75 ml
½ teaspoon ground
  cinnamon   2 ml

- After draining sweet potatoes, cut into smaller chunks and place in 4 to 5-quart (4 to 5 L) slow cooker.

- Add butter, brown sugar, orange juice, a little salt and a sprinkle of cinnamon and stir well.

- Cover and cook on LOW for 4 to 5 hours. Serves 4 to 6.

Hoppin' John

3 (15 ounce) cans black-eyed peas with liquid	3 (425 g)
1 onion, chopped	
1 (6 ounce) package parmesan-butter rice	170 g
2 cups cooked, chopped ham	280 g
2 tablespoons butter, melted	30 g

- In slow cooker, combine peas, onion, rice mix, ham, butter and 1¾ cups (425 ml) water and mix well.

- Cover and cook on LOW for 2 to 4 hours. Serves 6 to 8.

Spicy Spanish Rice

1½ cups white rice	280 g
1 (10 ounce) can diced tomatoes and green chilies	280 g
1 (15 ounce) can stewed tomatoes	425 g
1 (1 ounce) packet taco seasoning	30 g
1 large onion, chopped	

- Combine all ingredients plus 2 cups (500 ml) water in 5-quart (5 L) slow cooker and stir well.

- Cover and cook on LOW for 5 to 7 hours. (The flavor will go through the rice better if you stir 2 or 3 times during cooking time.) Serves 4.

TIP: Make this "a main dish" by slicing 1 pound (455 g) Polish sausage slices to rice mixture.

Delicious Risotto Rice

1½ cups Italian risotto rice	280 g
3 (14 ounce) cans chicken broth	3 (400 g)
3 tablespoons butter, melted	40 g
1½ cups sliced, fresh mushrooms	110 g
1 cup sliced celery	100 g

- Combine rice, broth, butter, mushrooms and celery in 4 to 5-quart (4 to 5 L) slow cooker.

- Cover and cook on LOW for 2 to 3 hours or until rice is tender. Serves 4 to 6.

Crunchy Couscous

When rice is boring, try couscous.

1 (10 ounce) box original plain couscous	280 g
2 cups sliced celery	200 g
1 red bell pepper, seeded, chopped	
1 yellow bell pepper, seeded, chopped	
1 (16 ounce) jar creamy alfredo sauce	455 g

- Combine couscous, celery, bell peppers, alfredo sauce and 1½ cups (375 ml) water in 5-quart (5 L) slow cooker and mix well.

- Cover and cook on LOW for 2 hours, stir once or twice.

- Check slow cooker to make sure celery and peppers are cooked, but still crunchy. Serves 4 to 6.

Carnival Couscous

1 (5.7 ounce) box herbed-chicken couscous	155 g
1 red bell pepper, seeded, julienned	
1 green bell pepper, seeded, julienned	
2 small yellow squash, sliced	
1 (16 ounce) package frozen mixed vegetables, thawed	455 g
1 (10 ounce) can French onion soup	280 g
¼ cup (½ stick) butter, melted	60 g
½ teaspoon seasoned salt	2 ml

- Combine all ingredients with 1½ cups (375 ml) water in sprayed slow cooker and mix well.

- Cover and cook on LOW for 2 to 4 hours. Serves 4.

St. Pat's Noodles

1 (12 ounce) package medium noodles	340 g
1 cup half-and-half cream	250 ml
1 (10 ounce) package frozen chopped spinach, thawed	280 g
6 tablespoons (¾ stick) butter, melted	85 g
2 teaspoons seasoned salt	10 ml
1½ cups shredded cheddar-Monterey Jack cheese	170 g

- Cook noodles according to package directions and drain.

- Place in 5 to 6-quart (5 to 6 L) slow cooker. Add half-and-half cream, spinach, butter and seasoned salt and stir until they blend well.

- Cover and cook on LOW for 2 to 3 hours.

- When ready to serve, fold in cheese. Serves 4.

Cheese-Spaghetti and Spinach

1 (7 ounce) box ready-cut spaghetti	200 g
2 tablespoons butter	30 g
1 (8 ounce) carton sour cream	230 g
1 cup shredded cheddar cheese	115 g
1 (8 ounce) package Monterey Jack cheese, divided	230 g
1 (12 ounce) package frozen, chopped spinach, thawed, well drained	340 g
1 (6 ounce) can cheddar french-fried onions, divided	170 g

- Cook spaghetti according to package directions, drain and stir in butter until it melts.

- Combine sour cream, cheddar cheese, half Monterey Jack cheese, spinach and half can onions in large bowl.

- Fold into spaghetti and spoon into sprayed slow cooker.

- Cover and cook on LOW for 2 to 4 hours.

- When ready to serve, sprinkle remaining Jack cheese and fried onion rings over top. Serves 4.

TIP: Squeeze spinach between paper towels to completely remove excess moisture.

Beef

Roasted, Smothered & Chopped

Beef Contents

Savory Steak.....................135
Swiss Steak.....................135
Pepper Steak.....................136
Spicy Swiss Steak...............137
Stroganoff......................138
Teriyaki Steak..................139
Mushroom-Round Steak..........140
O'Brian's Hash.................140
Italian Steak...................141
Cola Roast......................141
Beefy Onion Supper.............142
Beef Roulades...................143
Beef Tips over Noodles..........144
Beef Tips over Pasta............145
Pot Roast and Veggies...........146
Sweet-and-Sour Beef............147
Old-Time Pot Roast.............148
Beef Tips and Mushrooms Supreme..149
Herb-Crusted Beef Roast........150
Classic Beef Roast.............151
Mushroom Beef..................151
Beef Roast......................152
Smoked Brisket..................153
Good Brisket....................154
Sweet and Savory Brisket........154
Meat and Potatoes...............155

Beef Ribs and Gravy.............155
Brisket and Gravy...............156
Shredded Brisket for Sandwiches....157
The Best Ever Brisket...........158
A Different Corned Beef.........159
Justice with Short Ribs.........160
Beef and Noodles al Grande......161
Sauce for Fancy Meatballs.......162
Southwest Spaghetti.............162
Stuffed Cabbage.................163
Make-Believe Lasagna...........164
Mac 'n Cheese Supper...........165
Meat on the Table...............166
Jack's Meat Loaf................167
Hash Brown Dinner..............168
Fiesta Beef and Rice............169
Cowboy Feed.....................170
Cheeseburger Supper............171
Beef and Macaroni Supper.......172
Beef-Bean Medley...............173
Abundant Stuffed Shells.........174
Italy's Best....................175
Italian Tortellini..............176
Sloppy Joes.....................177
Beef and Gravy..................177
Special Hot Dog Supper.........178

Savory Steak

Great sauce with mashed potatoes

1½ pounds lean round
    steak   **680 g**
1 onion, halved,
    sliced
2 (10 ounce) cans
    golden
    mushroom soup   **2 (280 g)**
1½ cups hot, thick-
    and-chunky salsa **360 ml**

- Trim fat from steak and cut into serving-size pieces.

- Sprinkle with 1 teaspoon (5 ml) pepper and place in sprayed 5 to 6-quart (5 to 6 L) slow cooker.

- Place onion slices over steak.

- Combine mushroom soup and salsa in bowl and mix well. Spoon over steak and onions.

- Cover and cook on LOW for 7 to 8 hours. Serves 4 to 6.

Swiss Steak

1 - 1½ pounds boneless,
    round steak   **455 - 680 g**
½ teaspoon seasoned
    salt   **2 ml**
½ teaspoon seasoned
    pepper   **2 ml**
8 - 10 medium new
    (red) potatoes
    with peels, halved
1 cup baby carrots   **135 g**
1 onion, sliced
1 (15 ounce) can
    stewed tomatoes **425 g**
1 (12 ounce) jar beef
    gravy   **340 g**

- Cut steak in 6 to 8 serving-size pieces, season with seasoned salt and pepper and brown in non-stick skillet.

- Layer steak pieces, potatoes, carrots and onion in slow cooker.

- Combine tomatoes and beef gravy in bowl and spoon over vegetables.

- Cover and cook on LOW for 7 to 8 hours. Serves 4 to 6.

Pepper Steak

1½ pounds round steak	680 g
Canola oil	
¼ cup soy sauce	60 ml
1 onion, sliced	
1 teaspoon minced garlic	5 ml
1 teaspoon sugar	5 ml
¼ teaspoon ground ginger	1 ml
1 (15 ounce) can stewed tomatoes	425 g
2 green bell peppers, cored, seeded, julienned	
1 teaspoon beef bouillon granules	5 ml
1 tablespoon cornstarch	15 ml
Rice or noodles, cooked	

- Slice beef in strips, brown in skillet with a little oil and place in oval slow cooker.

- Combine soy sauce, onion, garlic, sugar and ginger in bowl and pour over beef.

- Cover and cook on LOW for 5 to 6 hours.

- Stir in tomatoes, bell peppers and bouillon and cook for an additional 1 hour.

- Combine cornstarch and ¼ cup water (60 ml) in cup and stir into cooker.

- Continue cooking until liquid thickens.

- Serve over rice or noodles. Serves 4 to 6.

Spicy Swiss Steak

**1½ pounds boneless,
beef round steak**   **680 g**
**4 ounces spicy
bratwurst**   **115 g**
2 small onions
**2 tablespoons
quick-cooking
tapioca**   **35 g**
**1 teaspoon dried
thyme**   **5 ml**
**2 (15 ounce) cans
Mexican stewed
tomatoes**   **2 (425 g)**
Noodles, cooked

- Trim fat from steak and cut into 4 serving-size pieces.

- Brown steak and bratwurst in skillet. Drain and place in sprayed 4 to 5-quart (4 to 5 L) slow cooker.

- Slice onions and separate into rings.

- Cover meat with onions and sprinkle with tapioca, thyme, a little salt and pepper. Pour stewed tomatoes over onion and seasonings.

- Cover and cook on LOW for 5 to 8 hours.

- Serve over noodles. Serves 4 to 6.

Stroganoff

2 pounds beef round steak	910 g
¾ cup flour, divided	90 g
½ teaspoon mustard	2 ml
2 onions, thinly sliced	
½ pound fresh mushrooms, sliced	230 g
1 (10 ounce) can beef broth	280 g
¼ cup dry white wine or cooking wine	60 ml
1 (8 ounce) carton sour cream	230 g

- Trim excess fat from steak and cut into 3-inch (8 cm) strips about ½-inch (1.2 cm) wide.

- Combine ½ cup (60 ml) flour, mustard and a little salt and pepper in bowl and toss with steak strips.

- Place strips in sprayed, oval slow cooker.

- Cover with onions and mushrooms. Add beef broth and wine. Cover and cook on LOW for 8 to 10 hours.

- Just before serving, combine sour cream and ¼ cup (60 ml) flour in bowl.

- Stir into cooker and cook for an additional 10 to 15 minutes or until stroganoff thickens slightly. Serves 4 to 6.

Teriyaki Steak

1½ - 2 pounds flank
   steak   680 - 910 g
1 (15 ounce) can
   sliced pineapple
   with juice   425 g
1 tablespoon
   marinade for
   chicken
   (Lea & Perrins)   15 ml
⅓ cup packed brown
   sugar   75 g
3 tablespoons soy
   sauce   45 ml
½ teaspoon ground
   ginger   2 ml
1 (14 ounce) can
   chicken broth   400 g
1 cup long grain
   converted rice   200 g

- Roll flank steak, tie in place and cut into 7 to 8 individual steaks.

- Combine ½ cup (125 ml) pineapple juice, Worcestershire, brown sugar, soy sauce and ginger in bowl large enough for marinade to cover individual steaks.

- Add steak rolls and marinate for 1 hour in sauce.

- Pour chicken broth into sprayed slow cooker.

- Add rice and ¾ cup (175 ml) water. Place steaks over rice and broth.

- Cover and cook on LOW for 8 to 10 hours. Serves 4 to 6.

Mushroom-Round Steak

1½ - 2 pounds round steak	680 - 910 g
1 (1 ounce) packet onion soup mix	30 g
½ cup dry red wine	125 ml
1 (8 ounce) carton fresh mushrooms, sliced	230 g
1 (10 ounce) can French onion soup	280 g

- Cut round steak in serving-size pieces and place in sprayed, oval slow cooker.

- Combine soup mix, red wine, mushrooms, French onion soup and ½ cup (125 ml) water in bowl, spoon over steak pieces.

- Cover and cook on LOW for 7 to 8 hours. Serves 4 to 6.

O'Brian's Hash

3 cups cooked, cubed beef roast	420 g
1 (28 ounce) package frozen hash browns with onions and peppers, thawed	795 g
Canola oil	
1 (16 ounce) jar salsa	455 g
1 tablespoon beef seasoning	15 ml
1 cup shredded cheddar-Jack cheese	116 g

- Place beef in large, sprayed slow cooker.

- Brown potatoes in little oil in large skillet. Stir in salsa and beef seasoning and transfer to slow cooker.

- Cover and cook on HIGH for 4 to 5 hours.

- When ready to serve, sprinkle cheese over top. Serves 4.

Italian Steak

1 pound round steak, cubed	455 g
2 cups fresh mushroom halves	145 g
1 (15 ounce) can Italian stewed tomatoes	425 g
1 (10 ounce) can beef broth	280 g
½ cup red wine	125 ml
2 teaspoons Italian seasoning	10 ml
3 tablespoons quick-cooking tapioca	50 g
Linguine, cooked	

- Place beef in sprayed 4 to 5-quart (4 to 5 L) slow cooker.

- Combine mushrooms, tomatoes, beef broth, wine, Italian seasoning, tapioca and a little salt and pepper in bowl. Pour over steak.

- Cover and cook on LOW for 8 to 10 hours.

- Serve over linguine. Serves 4.

Cola Roast

1 (4 pound) chuck roast	1.8 kg
1 (12 ounce) bottle chili sauce	340 g
1 onion, chopped	
1 (12 ounce) can cola	340 g
1 tablespoon Worcestershire sauce	15 ml

- Score roast in several places and fill each slit with a little salt and pepper.

- Sear roast in skillet on all sides. Place in 5-quart (5 L) slow cooker.

- Combine chili sauce, onion, cola and Worcestershire in bowl and mix well. Pour over roast.

- Cover and cook on LOW for 8 to 9 hours. Serves 6 to 8.

Beefy Onion Supper

**1 - 1½ pounds round
   steak**   **455 - 680 g**
1 onion
**2 cups fresh sliced
   mushrooms**   **145 g**
**1 (10 ounce) can
   French onion
   soup**   **280 g**
**1 (6 ounce) package
   herb stuffing mix**   **170 g**
**½ cup (1 stick) butter,
   melted**   **115 g**

- Cut beef into 5 to 6 serving-size pieces.

- Slice onion and separate into rings.

- Place steak pieces in oval slow cooker and top with onions and mushrooms.

- Pour soup over ingredients in cooker.

- Cover and cook on LOW for 7 to 9 hours.

- Just before serving, combine stuffing mix with seasoning packet, butter and ½ cup (125 ml) liquid from cooker and toss to mix.

- Place stuffing mixture on top of steak and increase heat to HIGH.

- Cover and cook for an additional 15 minutes or until stuffing is fluffy. Serves 4 to 6.

Beef Roulades

1½ pounds beef flank
    steak   **680 g**
5 slices bacon
¾ cup finely chopped
    onion   **120 g**
1 (4 ounce) can
    mushrooms pieces   **115 g**
1 tablespoon
    Worcestershire sauce   **15 ml**
⅓ cup Italian-seasoned
    breadcrumbs   **40 g**
1 (12 ounce) jar beef
    gravy   **340 g**

- Cut steak into 4 to 6 serving-size pieces. Cut bacon into small pieces and combine with onion, mushrooms, Worcestershire and breadcrumbs in bowl.

- Place about ½ cup (125 ml) onion mixture on each piece of steak.

- Roll meat and secure ends with toothpicks. Dry beef rolls with paper towels. In skillet, brown steak rolls and transfer to sprayed slow cooker.

- Pour gravy evenly over steaks to thoroughly moisten. Cover and cook on LOW for 7 to 9 hours. Serves 4 to 6.

TIP: This is really good served with mashed potatoes. Have you tried instant mashed potatoes as a time-saver?

Beef Tips over Noodles

½ cup plus 3 tablespoons
   flour, divided   **80 g**
3 pounds beef tips   **1.4 kg**
1 (8 ounce) carton fresh
   mushrooms, sliced   **230 g**
1 bunch fresh green
   onions, chopped
1 small red bell pepper,
   seeded, chopped
¼ cup ketchup   **70 g**
1 (14 ounce) can beef
   broth   **400 g**
1 tablespoon
   Worcestershire sauce   **15 ml**
Noodles, cooked

- Coat beef tips with ½ cup (60 g) flour in bowl and transfer to sprayed slow cooker.

- Add mushrooms, onion, bell pepper, ketchup, broth, Worcestershire sauce and a little salt and pepper.

- Cover and cook on LOW for 8 to 9 hours. About 1 hour before serving, turn heat to HIGH.

- Combine remaining flour with ¼ cup (60 ml) water in small bowl, stir into cooker and cook until liquid thickens.

- Serve over noodles. Serves 6 to 8.

Beef Tips over Pasta

2 - 2½ pounds lean, beef
    stew meat   910 g
2 cups frozen, small
    whole onions, thawed 320 g
1 green bell pepper,
    seeded
1 (6 ounce) jar pitted
    Greek olives or ripe
    olives   170 g
½ cup sun-dried tomatoes
    in oil, drained,
    chopped   30 g
1 (28 ounce) jar marinara
    sauce   795 g
1 (8 ounce) package pasta
    twirls, cooked   230 g

- Place beef and onions in sprayed 4 to 5-quart (4 to 5 L) slow cooker.

- Cut bell pepper in 1-inch (2.5 cm) cubes and add to slow cooker.

- Add olives and tomatoes and pour marinara sauce over top.

- Cover and cook on LOW for 8 to 10 hours.

- Serve over pasta twirls. Serves 4 to 6.

Pot Roast and Veggies

1 (2 pound) chuck roast	910 g
4 - 5 medium potatoes, peeled, quartered	
4 large carrots, quartered	
1 onion, quartered	
1 (14 ounce) can beef broth, divided	400 g
2 tablespoons cornstarch	15 g

- Trim fat from pieces of roast. Cut roast into 2 equal pieces.

- Brown pieces of roast in skillet. (Coat pieces with flour, salt and pepper if you'd like a little "breading" on the outside.)

- Place potatoes, carrots and onion in sprayed 4 to 5-quart (4 to 5 L) slow cooker and mix well. Place browned beef over vegetables.

- Pour 1½ cups (375 ml) broth over beef and vegetables. Save remaining broth and refrigerate.

- Cover and cook on LOW for 8 to 9 hours. About 5 minutes before serving, remove beef and vegetables with slotted spoon and place on serving platter. Cover to keep warm.

- Pour liquid from slow cooker into medium saucepan.

- Blend remaining ½ cup (125 ml) broth and cornstarch in bowl until smooth and add to liquid in saucepan. Boil for 1 minute and stir constantly.

- Serve gravy with roast and veggies and season with a little salt and pepper, if desired. Serves 4 to 6.

Sweet-and-Sour Beef

1 (2 pound) boneless chuck roast	910 g
½ cup flour	60 g
Canola oil	
1 onion, sliced	
½ cup chili sauce	135 g
¾ cup packed brown sugar	165 g
¼ cup red wine vinegar	60 ml
1 tablespoon Worcestershire sauce	15 ml
1 (16 ounce) package baby carrots	455 g

- Cut beef into 1-inch (2.5 cm) cubes and dredge in flour and a little salt and pepper.

- Brown beef in a little oil in skillet and place in sprayed slow cooker.

- Add remaining ingredients, except carrots, and 1 cup (250 ml) water.

- Cover and cook on LOW for 7 to 8 hours.

- Add carrots and cook for an additional 1 hour 30 minutes. Serves 4 to 6.

Old-Time Pot Roast

1 (2 - 2½) pound boneless
   rump roast   910 g
5 medium potatoes,
   peeled, quartered
1 (16 ounce) package
   peeled baby carrots   455 g
2 medium onions,
   quartered
1 (10 ounce) can golden
   mushroom soup   280 g
½ teaspoon dried basil   2 ml
½ teaspoon seasoned salt 2 ml

- Brown roast on all sides in large, non-stick skillet.

- Place potatoes, carrots and onions in sprayed 4 to 5-quart (4 to 5 L) slow cooker.

- Place browned roast on top of vegetables.

- Combine soup, basil and seasoned salt in bowl and pour mixture over meat and vegetables.

- Cover and cook on LOW for 9 to 11 hours. Serves 4 to 6.

TIP: *To serve, transfer roast and vegetables to serving plate. Stir juices remaining in slow cooker and spoon over roast and vegetables.*

Beef Tips and Mushrooms Supreme

2 (10 ounce) cans
  golden mushroom
  soup   2 (280 g)
1 (14 ounce) can
  beef broth   400 g
1 tablespoon beef
  seasoning   15 ml
2 (4 ounce) cans
  sliced mushrooms,
  drained   2 (115 g)
2 pounds round
  steak, cut in slices   910 g
Noodles
1 (8 ounce) carton
  sour cream   230 g

- Combine soups, beef broth, beef seasoning and sliced mushrooms in bowl. Place in slow cooker and stir to blend.

- Add slices of beef and stir well.

- Cover and cook on LOW for 4 to 5 hours.

- When ready to serve, cook noodles, drain, add salt and a little butter.

- Stir sour cream into sauce in slow cooker. Spoon sauce and beef over noodles. Serves 4 to 6.

Herb-Crusted Beef Roast

1 (2 - 3 pound) beef rump roast	910 g - 1.4 kg
¼ cup chopped fresh parsley	15 g
¼ cup chopped fresh oregano leaves	15 g
½ teaspoon dried rosemary leaves	2 ml
1 teaspoon minced garlic	5 ml
1 tablespoon canola oil	15 ml
6 slices thick-cut bacon	

- Rub roast with a little salt and pepper.

- Combine parsley, oregano, rosemary, garlic and oil in small bowl and press mixture on top and sides of roast.

- Place roast in slow cooker. Place bacon over top of beef and tuck ends under bottom.

- Cover and cook on LOW for 6 to 8 hours. Serves 4 to 6.

Classic Beef Roast

1 (3 - 4 pound) beef
  chuck roast   1.4 - 1.8 kg
1 (1 ounce) packet
  onion soup mix   30 g
2 (10 ounce) cans
  golden onion
  soup   2 (280 g)
3 - 4 medium potatoes,
  quartered

- Place roast in large, sprayed slow cooker.

- Sprinkle soup mix on roast and spoon on soup. Place potatoes around roast.

- Cover and cook on LOW for 7 to 8 hours or on HIGH for 4 hours. Serves 6 to 8.

Mushroom Beef

1 (10 ounce) can beefy
  mushroom soup   280 g
1 (10 ounce) can
  golden mushroom
  soup   280 g
1 (10 ounce) can
  French onion
  soup   280 g
⅓ cup seasoned
  breadcrumbs   40 g
2½ pounds lean beef
  stew meat   1.1 kg
Noodles, cooked

- Combine soups, ½ teaspoon (2 ml) pepper, breadcrumbs and ¾ cup (175 ml) water in 6-quart (6 L) slow cooker. Stir in beef cubes and mix well.

- Cover and cook on LOW for 8 to 9 hours.

- Serve over noodles. Serves 6 to 8.

Beef Roast

1 (4 pound) boneless	
rump roast	**1.8 kg**
½ cup flour, divided	**60 g**
1 (1 ounce) packet brown	
gravy mix	**30 g**
1 (1 ounce) packet beefy	
onion soup mix	**30 g**

- Cut roast in half (if needed to fit into cooker).

- Place roast in sprayed 5 to 6-quart (5 to 6 L) slow cooker and rub half of flour over roast.

- Combine remaining flour, gravy mix and soup mix in small bowl, gradually add 2 cups (500 ml) water and stir until they mix well. Pour over roast.

- Cover and cook on LOW for 7 to 8 hours or until roast is tender. Serves 6 to 8.

TIP: This is a great gravy to serve over mashed potatoes. Use instant mashed potatoes. They will never know the difference and will love the meal!

Smoked Brisket

1 (4 - 6 pound)
   trimmed brisket   1.8 - 2.7 kg
1 (4 ounce) bottle
   liquid smoke   115 g
Garlic salt
Celery salt
Worcestershire sauce
1 onion, chopped
1 (6 ounce) bottle
   barbecue sauce   170 g

- Place brisket in large shallow dish and pour liquid smoke over top.

- Sprinkle with garlic salt and celery salt. Cover and refrigerate overnight.

- Before cooking, drain liquid smoke and douse brisket with Worcestershire sauce.

- Place chopped onion in slow cooker and place brisket on top of onion.

- Cover and cook on LOW for 7 to 9 hours.

- With 1 hour left on cooking time, pour barbecue sauce over brisket and cook for an additional 1 hour. Serves 6 to 8.

Good Brisket

½ cup packed brown
    sugar   110 g
1 tablespoon Cajun
    seasoning   15 ml
2 teaspoons lemon pepper 10 ml
1 tablespoon
    Worcestershire sauce   15 ml
1 (3 - 4 pound)
    trimmed beef
    brisket   1.4 - 1.8 kg

- Combine brown sugar, seasoning, lemon pepper and Worcestershire in small bowl and spread on brisket.

- Place brisket in sprayed, oval slow cooker.

- Cover and cook on LOW for 6 to 8 hours. Serves 6 to 8.

Sweet and Savory Brisket

1 (3 - 4 pound) trimmed
    beef brisket,
    halved   1.4 - 1.8 kg
⅓ cup grape or plum
    jelly   110 g
1 cup ketchup   270 g
1 (1 ounce) packet dry
    onion soup mix   30 g

- Place half of brisket in slow cooker.

- Combine jelly, ketchup, onion soup mix and ¾ teaspoon (4 ml) pepper in saucepan and heat just enough to mix well. Spread half over brisket.

- Top with remaining brisket and jelly-soup mixture.

- Cover and cook on LOW for 8 to 9 hours. Slice brisket and serve with cooking juices. Serves 6 to 8.

Meat and Potatoes

4 medium potatoes,
  peeled, sliced
1¼ pounds lean ground
  beef, browned   570 g
1 onion, sliced
1 (10 ounce) can cream
  of mushroom soup   280 g
1 (10 ounce) can
  vegetable beef soup   280 g

- Layer all ingredients with a little salt and pepper in large slow cooker.

- Cover and cook on LOW for 5 to 6 hours. Serves 4 to 6.

Beef Ribs and Gravy

4 pounds beef short ribs   1.8 kg
1 onion, sliced
1 (12 ounce) jar beef
  gravy   340 g
1 (1 ounce) packet beef
  gravy mix   30 g

- Place beef ribs in sprayed 6-quart (6 L) slow cooker. Cover with onion and sprinkle with 1 teaspoon (5 ml) pepper.

- Combine beef gravy and dry gravy mix in small bowl and pour over ribs and onion.

- Cover and cook on LOW for 9 to 11 hours. (The ribs must cook this long on LOW to tenderize.) Serves 4 to 6.

TIP: Serve with hot mashed potatoes and gravy.

Brisket and Gravy

1 (3 - 4 pound)
  trimmed beef
  brisket   1.4 - 1.8 kg
¼ cup chili sauce   70 g
1 (1 ounce) packet
  herb-garlic soup
  mix   30 g
2 tablespoons
  Worcestershire
  sauce   30 ml
3 tablespoons
  cornstarch   25 g
Mashed potatoes

- Place beef brisket in sprayed 5 to 6-quart (5 to 6 L) slow cooker. Cut to fit if necessary.

- Combine chili sauce, soup mix, Worcestershire and 1½ cups (375 ml) water in bowl and pour over brisket.

- Cover and cook on LOW for 9 to 11 hours.

- Remove brisket and keep warm. Pour juices into 2-cup (500 ml) glass measuring cup and skim fat.

- Combine cornstarch and ¼ cup (60 ml) water in saucepan. Add 1½ cups (375 ml) juices and cook, while stirring constantly, until gravy thickens.

- Slice beef thinly across grain and serve with mashed potatoes and gravy. Serves 6 to 8.

Shredded Brisket for Sandwiches

2 teaspoons onion powder	10 ml
1 teaspoon minced garlic	5 ml
1 (3 - 4 pound) beef brisket	1.4 - 1.8 kg
1 tablespoon liquid smoke	15 ml
1 (16 ounce) bottle barbecue sauce	455 g
Kaiser rolls or hamburger buns	

- Combine onion powder, minced garlic and liquid smoke in bowl and rub over brisket.

- Place brisket in large, sprayed slow cooker. Add ⅓ cup (75 ml) water to cooker.

- Cover and cook on LOW for 6 to 8 hours or until brisket is tender.

- Remove brisket, cool and reserve ½ cup (125 ml) cooking juices.

- Shred brisket with 2 forks and place in large saucepan. Add ½ cup (125 ml) cooking juices and barbecue sauce and heat thoroughly.

- Make sandwiches with kaiser rolls or hamburger buns. Serves 6 to 8.

The Best Ever Brisket

1 (3 - 4) pound fresh,
   trimmed brisket   **1.4 - 1.8 kg**
3 onions, sliced
1 (8 ounce) package
   fresh mushrooms,
   halved   **230 g**
1 teaspoon seasoned
   salt   **5 ml**
1 (12 ounce) can beer
   (not light)   **340 g**
1 cup chili sauce   **270 g**
1 (4 ounce) can
   chopped green
   chilies   **115 g**

- If necessary, trim brisket to fit into large, sprayed oval slow cooker. Layer onions and mushrooms in bottom of slow cooker and sprinkle with seasoned salt. Top with brisket.

- Combine beer, chili sauce and green chilies in medium bowl and mix well. Pour mixture over brisket in slow cooker.

- Cover and cook on LOW heat for 10 to 12 hours or on HIGH for 5 to 6 hours. When ready to serve, remove brisket from slow cooker and thinly slice meat across the grain.

- Place brisket on serving platter and place onions and mushrooms on top of brisket. Serves 8 to 10.

A Different Corned Beef

2 onions, sliced
Lemon pepper
1 (3 - 4 pound)
    seasoned corned
    beef   **1.4 - 1.8 kg**

- Place sliced onions in large slow cooker. Add 1 cup (250 ml) water. Sprinkle lemon pepper liberally over corned beef and place on top on onion. Cover and cook on LOW for 7 to 9 hours.

- Remove corned beef from slow cooker and place in ovenproof pan. Preheat oven to 375° (190° C).

Glaze:

¼ cup honey   **85 g**
¼ cup frozen orange
    juice concentrate,
    thawed   **60 ml**
1 tablespoon mustard   **15 ml**

- Combining all ingredients and spoon over corned beef. Bake for 30 minutes and baste occasionally with glaze before serving. Serves 6 to 8.

Justice with Short Ribs

Flour

3 pounds beef short ribs	1.4 kg
3 tablespoons olive oil	45 ml
1 onion, thinly sliced	
½ cup chili sauce	135 g
¼ cup packed brown sugar	55 g
3 tablespoons vinegar	45 ml
½ teaspoon dry mustard	2 ml
1 teaspoon chili powder	5 ml
2 tablespoons flour	15 g

- Coat ribs with lots of salt and pepper; then dredge in flour, coating well. Brown short ribs in oil in large skillet over medium-high heat until they are light brown.

- Place onion, chili sauce, brown sugar, vinegar, mustard and chili powder in sprayed slow cooker; mix thoroughly.

- Place browned ribs into slow cooker. Cover and cook on LOW for 6 to 8 hours.

- Remove ribs to serving platter and turn slow cooker to HIGH heat. Combine remaining 2 tablespoons flour with ¾ cup (175 ml) water in bowl and stir into sauce in slow cooker.

- Cook for 10 minutes or until mixture thickens. When serving, spoon sauce over ribs. Serves 6.

Beef and Noodles al Grande

1½ pounds lean
   ground beef   680 g
1 (16 ounce) package
   frozen onions and
   bell peppers,
   thawed   455 g
1 (16 ounce) box
   Velveeta® cheese,
   cubed   455 g
2 (15 ounce) cans
   Mexican stewed
   tomatoes with
   liquid   425 g
2 (15 ounce) cans
   whole kernel corn,
   drained   2 (425 g)
1 (8 ounce) package
   medium egg
   noodles   230 g
1 cup shredded
   cheddar cheese   115 g
Fresh parsley or
   green onions

- Brown ground beef in skillet and drain fat.

- Place beef in sprayed 5 to 6-quart (5 to 6 L) slow cooker, add onions and peppers, cheese, tomatoes, corn and about 1 teaspoon (5 ml) salt and mix well.

- Cover and cook on LOW for 4 to 5 hours.

- Cook noodles according to package direction, drain and fold into beef-tomato mixture. Cook for an additional 30 minutes to heat thoroughly.

- When ready to serve, top with cheddar cheese, several sprinkles of chopped fresh parsley or chopped fresh green onions. Serves 4 to 6.

Sauce for Fancy Meatballs

1 (16 ounce) can whole-berry cranberry sauce	455 g
1 cup ketchup	270 g
⅔ cup packed brown sugar	150 g
½ cup beef broth	125 ml
1 (18 ounce) package frozen meatballs, thawed	510 g

- Combine cranberry sauce, ketchup, brown sugar and broth in large slow cooker.

- Turn heat to HIGH and let mixture come to a boil for 30 minutes to 1 hour. Place package of thawed meatballs in sauce.

- Cover and cook on LOW for 2 hours.

- Remove meatballs to serving dish with slotted spoon. Insert toothpicks for easy pick up.

- Serve as an appetizer, for supper or buffet pick-up food. Serves 4 to 6.

Southwest Spaghetti

1½ pounds lean ground beef	680 g
2½ teaspoons chili powder	12 ml
1 (15 ounce) can tomato sauce	425 g
1 (7 ounce) package spaghetti	200 g
1 heaping tablespoon beef seasoning	15 ml
Shredded cheddar-Jack cheese	

- Brown ground beef in skillet until no longer pink. Place in 4 to 5-quart (4 to 5 L) slow cooker.

- Add chili powder, tomato sauce, spaghetti, 2⅓ cups (575 ml) water and beef seasoning and mix well.

- Cover and cook on LOW for 6 to 7 hours.

- When ready to serve, cover with lots of shredded cheddar-Jack cheese. Serves 4 to 6.

Stuffed Cabbage

**10 - 12 large cabbage
   leaves**

**1½ pounds lean ground
   beef**   **680 g**

½ cup brown rice   **95 g**

1 egg, beaten

**¼ teaspoon ground
   cinnamon**   **1 ml**

**1 (15 ounce) can tomato
   sauce**   **425 g**

- Wash cabbage leaves, place in saucepan of boiling water and turn off heat. Soak for about 5 minutes.

- Remove leaves, drain and cool.

- Combine beef, rice, egg, 1 teaspoon (5 ml) salt, ½ teaspoon (2 ml) pepper and cinnamon in bowl and mix well.

- Place 2 tablespoons (30 ml) beef mixture on each cabbage leaf and roll tightly. (If you can't get 10 to 12 large leaves, put 2 together to make 1 large leaf.)

- Stack rolls in sprayed, oval slow cooker and pour tomato sauce over rolls.

- Cover and cook on HIGH for 1 hour, lower heat to LOW and cook for an additional 6 to 7 hours. Serves 4 to 6.

Make-Believe Lasagna

1 pound lean ground
  beef   455 g
1 onion, chopped
½ teaspoon garlic
  powder   2 ml
1 (18 ounce) can
  spaghetti sauce   510 g
½ teaspoon ground
  oregano   2 ml
6 - 8 lasagna noodles,
  divided
1 (12 ounce) carton
  cottage cheese,
  divided   340 g
½ cup grated parmesan
  cheese, divided   50 g
1 (12 ounce) package
  shredded mozzarella
  cheese, divided   340 g

- Brown ground beef and onion in large skillet. Add garlic powder, spaghetti sauce and oregano. Cook just until thoroughly warm.

- Spoon layer of meat sauce in sprayed, oval slow cooker. Add layer lasagna noodles (break to fit slow cooker).

- Top with layer of half remaining meat sauce, half cottage cheese, half parmesan cheese and half mozzarella cheese. Repeat layers and start with more lasagna noodles.

- Cover and cook on LOW for 6 to 8 hours. Serves 4 to 6.

Mac 'n Cheese Supper

1½ pounds lean ground beef	680 g
2 (7 ounce) packages macaroni and cheese dinners	2 (200 g)
1 (15 ounce) can whole kernel corn, drained	425 g
1½ cups shredded Monterey Jack cheese	170 g

- Sprinkle ground beef with ½ teaspoon (2 ml) salt, brown in skillet until no longer pink and drain.

- Prepare macaroni and cheese according to package directions.

- Spoon in beef, macaroni and corn in sprayed 5-quart (5 L) slow cooker and mix well.

- Cover and cook on LOW for 4 to 5 hours.

- When ready to serve, sprinkle Jack cheese over top and leave in cooker until cheese melts. Serves 4 to 6.

Meat on the Table

1½ - 2 pounds lean ground beef	680 - 910 g
1 (1 ounce) packet beefy onion soup mix	30 g
⅔ cup quick-cooking oats	55 g
2 eggs	
1 (12 ounce) bottle chili sauce, divided	340 g

- Combine beef, onion soup mix, oats, eggs, ¾ cup (204 g) chili sauce and 1 teaspoon (5 ml) black pepper in bowl and mix well.

- Shape meat mixture into round ball, place in sprayed slow cooker and pat down into loaf shape.

- Cover and cook on LOW for 3 to 4 hours.

- Before last half hour of cooking time, spread remaining chili sauce over top of loaf and continue cooking.

- Use foil handles to lift meat loaf out of slow cooker. Serves 4 to 6.

Jack's Meat Loaf

2 pounds lean ground
    beef   910 g
2 eggs
½ cup chili sauce   135 g
1¼ cups seasoned
    breadcrumbs   150 g
1 (8 ounce) package
    shredded Monterey
    Jack cheese, divided   230 g

- Combine beef, eggs, chili sauce and breadcrumbs in bowl and mix well.

- Shape half beef mixture into flat loaf and place in sprayed slow cooker.

- Sprinkle half cheese over meat loaf and press into meat.

- Form remaining meat mixture in same shape as first layer, place over cheese and seal seams.

- Cover and cook on LOW for 6 to 7 hours.

- When ready to serve, sprinkle remaining cheese over loaf and leave in cooker until cheese melts.

- Carefully remove loaf with foil handles and place on serving plate. Serves 4 to 6.

Hash Brown Dinner

1½ pounds lean ground chuck, browned	680 g
1 (1 ounce) packet brown gravy mix	30 g
1 (15 ounce) can cream-style corn	425 g
1 (15 ounce) can whole kernel corn	425 g
1 (8 ounce) package shredded cheddar cheese, divided	230 g
1 (18 ounce) package frozen hash browns, partially thawed	510 g
1 (10 ounce) can golden mushroom soup	280 g
1 (5 ounce) can evaporated milk	145 g

- Place browned beef in sprayed slow cooker and toss with dry brown gravy.

- Add cream-style corn and whole kernel corn and cover with half cheddar cheese.

- Top with hash browns and remaining cheese.

- Combine mushroom soup and evaporated milk in bowl. Mix well and pour over hash browns and cheese.

- Cover and cook on LOW for 6 to 8 hours. Serves 4 to 6.

Fiesta Beef and Rice

1½ pounds lean ground
    beef   680 g
1 (15 ounce) can Mexican
    stewed tomatoes   425 g
1 (7 ounce) box
    beef-flavored rice mix 200 g
1 (11 ounce) can
    Mexicorn®, drained   310 g
Salsa

- Sprinkle salt and pepper over ground beef and shape into small patties.

- Place in sprayed 5-quart (5 L) oval slow cooker.

- Combine stewed tomatoes, rice, corn and 2 cups (500 ml) water in bowl and mix well. Spoon over beef patties.

- Cover and cook on LOW for 4 to 5 hours.

- When ready to serve, place large spoonful of salsa on each serving. Serves 4 to 6.

Cowboy Feed

1½ pounds lean ground beef	680 g
2 onions, coarsely chopped	
5 medium potatoes, peeled, sliced	
1 (15 ounce) can kidney beans, rinsed, drained	425 g
1 (15 ounce) can pinto beans, drained	425 g
1 (15 ounce) can Mexican stewed tomatoes	425 g
1 (10 ounce) can tomato soup	280 g
½ teaspoon basil	2 ml
½ teaspoon oregano	2 ml
2 teaspoons minced garlic	10 ml

- Sprinkle beef with some salt and pepper, brown in skillet and drain.

- Place onions in slow cooker and spoon beef over onions.

- On top of beef, layer potatoes, kidney and pinto beans.

- Pour stewed tomatoes and tomato soup over beans and potatoes and sprinkle with basil, oregano and garlic.

- Cover and cook on LOW for 7 to 8 hours. Serves 4 to 6.

Cheeseburger Supper

1 (5 ounce) box bacon and cheddar scalloped potatoes	145 g
⅓ cup milk	75 ml
¼ cup (½ stick) butter, melted	60 g
1½ pounds lean ground beef	680 g
1 onion, coarsely chopped	
Canola oil	
1 (15 ounce) can whole kernel corn with liquid	425 g
1 (8 ounce) package shredded cheddar cheese	230 g

- Place scalloped potatoes in sprayed slow cooker.

- Pour 2¼ cups (560 ml) boiling water, milk and butter over potatoes.

- Brown ground beef and onion in little oil in skillet, drain and spoon over potatoes. Top with corn.

- Cover and cook on LOW for 6 to 7 hours.

- When ready to serve, sprinkle cheese over corn. Serves 4 to 6.

Beef and Macaroni Supper

1 (10 ounce) package macaroni, cooked, drained	280 g
3 tablespoons canola oil	45 ml
1½ pounds lean ground beef, browned, drained	680 g
1 onion, chopped	
3 ribs celery, chopped	
2 (10 ounce) cans tomato soup	2 (280 g)
1 (6 ounce) can tomato paste	170 g
1 teaspoon beef bouillon granules	5 ml
1 (8 ounce) package cubed Velveeta® cheese	230 g

- Toss cooked macaroni with oil to make sure macaroni does not stick together.

- Place in sprayed slow cooker.

- Add beef, onion, celery, tomato soup, tomato paste, beef bouillon and ⅔ cup (150 ml) water and stir to mix well.

- Cover and cook on LOW for 4 to 6 hours. Before last hour of cooking time, stir in cubed cheese. Serves 4 to 6.

Beef-Bean Medley

1 pound lean ground
    beef   455 g
1 onion, chopped
6 slices bacon, cooked,
    crumbled
2 (15 ounce) cans
    pork and beans   2 (425 g)
1 (15 ounce) can
    butter beans,
    rinsed, drained   425 g
1 (15 ounce) can
    kidney beans,
    rinsed, drained   425 g
½ cup ketchup   135 g
½ cup packed brown
    sugar   110 g
3 tablespoons
    vinegar   45 ml
1 (13 ounce) bag
    original corn
    chips   370 g
1 (8 ounce) package
    shredded cheddar
    cheese   230 g

- Brown ground beef and onion in skillet, drain and transfer to sprayed 4 to 5-quart (4 to 5 L) slow cooker.

- Add bacon and all 4 cans of beans.

- Combine ketchup, brown sugar and vinegar in bowl. Add to cooker and stir.

- Cover and cook on LOW for 4 to 6 hours.

- When ready to serve, spoon over corn chips and sprinkle cheese over top. Serves 4 to 6.

Abundant Stuffed Shells

20 - 22 jumbo pasta shells	
¾ pound lean ground beef, browned, drained	340 g
½ cup finely chopped onion	80 g
1 cup shredded cheddar cheese	115 g
⅓ cup seasoned breadcrumbs	40 g
1 teaspoon minced garlic	5 ml
½ teaspoon Italian seasoning	2 ml
1 egg, beaten	
2 (26 ounce) jar spaghetti sauce	2 (740 g)
½ cup shredded mozzarella cheese	60 g

- Cook pasta shells for 7 minutes in boiling water in saucepan (they need only to be partially cooked), drain and place on sheet of wax paper.

- Combine beef, onion, cheddar cheese, breadcrumbs, garlic, seasoning and egg in bowl. Carefully stuff partially cooked pasta shells with spoonful of meat mixture.

- Pour 1 jar spaghetti sauce in sprayed slow cooker. Transfer stuffed shells on top of sauce. Pour remaining sauce evenly over pasta. Sprinkle with mozzarella cheese.

- Cover and cook on LOW heat 4 to 5 hours. Do not over cook. Serves 4 to 6.

Italy's Best

2 pounds lean ground beef	910 g
1 large onion, chopped	
1 green bell pepper, seeded, chopped	
1 teaspoon minced garlic	5 ml
1 (15 ounce) can tomato sauce	425 g
1 (15 ounce) can Italian stewed tomatoes	425 g
2 teaspoons Italian seasoning	10 ml
1 (16 ounce) package penne pasta	455 g
1 (10 ounce) package frozen, chopped spinach, thawed	280 g
1 (12 ounce) package shredded mozzarella cheese	340 g

- Brown and cook ground beef, onion, bell pepper and garlic in large skillet for about 15 minutes. Drain and place mixture in sprayed slow cooker.

- Stir in tomato sauce, stewed tomatoes, Italian seasoning and a little salt and pepper. Cover and cook on LOW for 7 to 8 hours or on HIGH for 3 hours 30 minutes.

- Cook pasta according to package directions and drain. Last 30 minutes of cooking time, turn heat to HIGH (if cooking on LOW) stir in pasta, spinach and cheese and continue cooking. Serves 6 to 8.

Italian Tortellini

½ pound ground round
   steak   230 g
1 (1 pound) package
   bulk Italian sausage   455 g
1 (15 ounce) carton
   refrigerated marinara
   sauce   425 g
1 (15 ounce) can Italian
   stewed tomatoes with
   liquid   425 g
1½ cups sliced fresh
   mushrooms   110 g
1 (9 ounce) package
   refrigerated cheese
   tortellini   255g
1½ cups shredded
   mozzarella cheese   170 g

- Brown and cook ground beef and sausage in large skillet for about 10 minutes on medium-low heat and drain.

- Combine meat mixture, marinara sauce, tomatoes and mushrooms in 4 to 5-quart (4 to 5 L) slow cooker.

- Cover and cook on LOW 6 to 8 hours.

- Stir in tortellini and sprinkle with mozzarella cheese.

- Turn cooker to HIGH and continue cooking for an additional 10 to 15 minutes or until tortellini is tender. Serves 4 to 6.

Sloppy Joes

3 pounds ground beef	1.4 kg
1 tablespoon minced garlic	15 ml
1 large onion, finely chopped	
2 ribs celery, chopped	
¼ cup packed brown sugar	55 g
3½ tablespoons mustard	55 g
1 tablespoon chili powder	15 ml
1½ cups ketchup	410 g
3 tablespoons Worcestershire sauce	45 ml

- Brown beef, garlic and onion in very large skillet and drain.

- Combine celery, brown sugar, mustard, chili powder, ketchup and Worcestershire in sprayed 5-quart (5 L) slow cooker. Stir in meat mixture.

- Cover and cook on LOW heat for 6 to 7 hours. Serves 6 to 8.

TIP: This will make enough to fill 16 to 18 hamburger buns.

Beef and Gravy

2 pounds sirloin steak or thick round steak	910 g
Canola oil	
1 (1 ounce) packet onion soup mix	30 g
1 (10 ounce) can golden mushroom soup	280 g
1 (4 ounce) can sliced mushrooms, drained	115 g
Noodles, cooked	

- Cut steak in ½-inch (1.2 cm) pieces. Brown beef in skillet in a little oil and place in 5 to 6-quart (5 to 6L) slow cooker.

- Combine onion soup mix, mushroom soup, mushrooms and ½ cup (125 ml) water in bowl and mix well. Spoon over top of beef.

- Cover and cook on LOW for 7 to 8 hours. Serve over noodles. Serves 4 to 6.

Special Hot Dog Supper

1 pound beef wieners	455 g
2 (15 ounce) cans chili without beans	2 (425 g)
1 onion, finely chopped	
1 (10 ounce) can cheddar cheese soup	280 g
1 (10 ounce) can fiesta nacho cheese soup	280 g
1 (7 ounce) can chopped green chilies, drained	200 g
Corn chips or tortilla chips	

- Cut wieners in ½-inch (1.2 cm) pieces and place in sprayed slow cooker.

- Combine chili, onion, cheese soup, nacho cheese soup and green chilies in saucepan. (Omit green chilies if serving to kids.)

- Heat just enough to mix ingredients well. Spoon over wieners.

- Cover and cook on LOW for 1 hour 30 minutes to 2 hours.

- Serve over bowl of small corn chips or crisp tortilla chips slightly crushed. Serves 4 to 6.

Chicken & Turkey

Honey-Baked, Oranged & Noodled

Chicken & Turkey Contents

Chicken Olé 182
Chicken for the Gods 182
Apricot Chicken 183
Broccoli-Rice Chicken 183
Artichoke-Chicken Pasta. 184
Chicken Curry over Rice. 185
Bacon-Wrapped Chicken. 185
Broccoli-Cheese Chicken 186
Cream Cheese Chicken 186
Chicken and Noodles 187
Chicken and Pasta. 188
Chicken and Vegetables 189
Chicken Delicious. 190
Chicken Delight 191
Chicken Dinner. 192
Chicken-Supper Ready 192
Chicken Fajitas 193
Chicken for Supper. 194
Chicken-Ready Supper 194
Chicken Marseilles 195
Chicken Breast Deluxe 196
Chicken Supper. 197
Chow Mein Chicken 198
Classy Chicken Dinner 199
Creamy Chicken and Potatoes. 199
Creamed Chicken 200
Creamed Chicken and Vegetables 201
Creamy Salsa Chicken 202
Delightful Chicken and Veggies 202
Slow Cooker Cordon Bleu 203
Delicious Chicken Pasta 204
Farmhouse Supper 205

Golden Chicken Dinner. 206
Hawaiian Chicken. 207
Imperial Chicken. 207
Here's the Stuff. 208
Mushroom Chicken. 209
Orange Chicken 210
Oregano Chicken 210
Quick-Fix Chicken 211
Picante Chicken 211
Perfect Chicken Breasts 212
Russian Chicken 213
So-Good Chicken 213
Winter Dinner 214
Savory Chicken Fettuccini 215
Scrumptious Chicken Breasts 216
Smothered Chicken Breasts. 217
Southwestern Chicken Pot 218
Sweet-and-Sour Chicken. 218
Sunday Chicken 219
Tasty Chicken-Rice and Veggies 220
Honey-Baked Chicken 221
Tangy Chicken 221
Chicken with Orange Sauce 222
Tasty Chicken and Veggies 223
"Baked" Chicken 223
Saffron Rice and Chicken 224
Lemon Chicken. 225
Chicken Coq au Vin 226
Chicken Cacciatore. 227
Taco Chicken 228
Tangy Chicken Legs 228
Monterey Bake 229

Chicken & Turkey Contents

Chicken and Stuffing. 230
Chicken and Everything Good 231
Chicken Alfredo 232
Sweet and Spicy Chicken 233
Maple-Plum Glazed Turkey Breast . . .233
Southern Chicken 234
Italian Chicken 235
Asparagus-Cheese Chicken. 236
Cheesy Chicken and Noodles 237
Stupendous Rice and Chicken. 238

Three Hour Chicken 239
Arroz con Pollo. 239
Yes to This Chicken 240
Turkey Bake 241
Turkey Loaf 242
Turkey Spaghetti. 243
Turkey Cassoulet 244
Colorful Rice and Turkey 245
Sausage and Rice 246

Chicken Olé

6 boneless, skinless chicken
   breast halves
1 (8 ounce) package
   cream cheese,
   softened   230g
1 (16 ounce) jar salsa   455 g
2 teaspoons cumin   10 ml
1 bunch fresh green
   onions with tops,
   chopped

- Pound chicken breasts to flatten. Beat cream cheese in bowl until smooth, add salsa, cumin and onions and mix gently.

- Place heaping spoonfuls of cream cheese mixture on each chicken breast and roll. (There will be leftover cream cheese mixture.)

- Place chicken breast seam side-down in sprayed slow cooker. Spoon remaining cream cheese mixture over each chicken roll.

- Cover and cook on LOW for 5 to 6 hours. Serves 4 to 6.

Chicken for the Gods

1¾ cups flour   180 g
Scant 2 tablespoons dry
   mustard   30 ml
6 boneless, skinless
   chicken breast halves
2 tablespoons canola oil   30 ml
1 (10 ounce) can
   chicken-rice soup   280 g

- Place flour and mustard in shallow bowl and dredge chicken to coat all sides.

- Brown chicken breasts in oil in skillet. Place all breasts in 6-quart (6 L) oval slow cooker.

- Pour chicken and rice soup over chicken and add about ¼ cup (60 ml) water.

- Cover and cook on LOW for 6 to 7 hours. Serves 4 to 6.

Apricot Chicken

6 boneless, skinless
   chicken breasts
   halves
1 (12 ounce) jar apricot
   preserves   340g
1 (8 ounce) bottle
   Catalina dressing   230 g
1 (1 ounce) packet onion
   soup mix   30 g

• Place chicken in sprayed
  6-quart (6 L) slow cooker.

• Combine apricot preserves,
  Catalina dressing, onion soup
  mix and ¼ cup (60 ml) water
  and stir well. Cover chicken
  breasts with sauce mixture.

• Cover and cook on LOW for
  5 to 6 hours. Serves 4 to 6.

Broccoli-Rice Chicken

1¼ cups converted rice   250 g
2 pounds boneless,
   skinless chicken
   breast halves   680 g
Dried parsley
1 (2 ounce) packet
   cream of broccoli
   soup mix   60 g
1 (14 ounce) can
   chicken broth   400 g

• Place rice in lightly sprayed
  slow cooker. Cut chicken into
  slices and place over rice.

• Sprinkle with parsley and a
  little pepper.

• Combine soup mix, chicken
  broth and 1 cup (250 ml) water
  in saucepan. Heat just enough
  to mix well. Pour over chicken
  and rice.

• Cover and cook on LOW for
  6 to 8 hours. Serves 4 to 6.

Artichoke-Chicken Pasta

1½ pounds boneless, skinless chicken breast tenders	680 g
1 (15 ounce) can artichoke hearts, quartered	425 g
¾ cup chopped, roasted, red peppers	110 g
1 (8 ounce) package American cheese, shredded	230 g
1 tablespoon marinade for chicken (Lea & Perrins)	15 ml
1 (10 ounce) can cream of chicken soup	280 g
1 (8 ounce) package shredded cheddar cheese	230 g
4 cups hot, cooked bow-tie pasta	300 g

- Combine chicken tenders, artichoke, roasted peppers, American cheese, Worcestershire sauce and soup in slow cooker and mix well.

- Cover and cook on LOW for 6 to 8 hours. About 20 minutes before serving, fold in cheddar cheese, hot pasta and a little salt and pepper. Serves 4.

Chicken Curry over Rice

3 large boneless, skinless chicken
  breast halves
½ cup chicken broth   125 ml
1 (10 ounce) can cream of
  chicken soup   280 g
1 onion, coarsely chopped
1 red bell pepper, seeded,
  julienned
¼ cup golden raisins   40 g
1½ teaspoons curry
  powder   7 ml
¼ teaspoon ground ginger 1 ml
Rice, cooked

- Cut chicken into thin strips and
  place in sprayed 5 to 6-quart
  (5 to 6 L) slow cooker.

- Combine broth, soup, onion, bell
  pepper, raisins, curry powder
  and ginger in bowl and mix
  well. Pour over chicken.

- Cover and cook on LOW for
  3 to 4 hours. Serve over rice.
  Serves 4.

Bacon-Wrapped Chicken

1 (2.5 ounce) jar
  dried beef   70 g
6 boneless, skinless
  chicken breast
  halves
6 slices bacon
2 (10 ounce) cans
  golden
  mushroom soup   2 (280 g)
1 (6 ounce) package
  parmesan-butter
  rice, cooked   170 g

- Place dried beef sliced in 5-quart
  (5 L) slow cooker.

- Roll each chicken breast half in
  slice of bacon and place over
  dried beef.

- Heat soup and ⅓ cup (75 ml)
  water in saucepan just enough to
  mix well and pour over chicken.

- Cover and cook on LOW for
  7 to 8 hours.

- Serve over rice. Serves 4 to 6.

Broccoli-Cheese Chicken

4 boneless, skinless
   chicken breast
   halves
2 tablespoons butter,
   melted   30 g
1 (10 ounce) can
   broccoli-cheese soup   280 g
¼ cup milk   60 ml
1 (10 ounce) package
   frozen broccoli spears 280 g
Rice, cooked

- Dry chicken breasts with paper towels and place in sprayed, oval slow cooker.

- Combine melted butter, soup and milk in bowl and spoon over chicken. Cover and cook on LOW for 4 to 6 hours.

- Remove cooker lid and place broccoli over chicken. Cover and cook for an additional 1 hour. Serve over rice. Serves 4.

Cream Cheese Chicken

4 boneless, skinless
   chicken breast
   halves
2 tablespoons butter,
   melted   30 g
1 (10 ounce) can cream
   of mushroom soup   280 g
2 tablespoons dry Italian
   salad dressing   30 ml
½ cup sherry   125 ml
1 (8 ounce) package
   cream cheese, cubed   230 g
Noodles, cooked

- Wash chicken breasts, dry with paper towels and brush melted butter over chicken.

- Place in sprayed, oval slow cooker and add remaining ingredients.

- Cover and cook on LOW for 6 to 7 hours. Serve over noodles. Serves 4.

Chicken and Noodles

2 pounds boneless,
  skinless chicken
  breast halves   **910 g**
¼ cup cornstarch   **30 g**
⅓ cup soy sauce   **75 ml**
2 onions, chopped
3 ribs celery, sliced
  diagonally
1 red bell pepper,
  seeded, julienned
2 (14 ounce) cans
  mixed Chinese
  vegetables,
  drained   **2 (400 g)**
¼ cup molasses   **60 ml**
Chow mein noodles

- Place chicken breasts and 2 cups (500 ml) water in sprayed slow cooker.

- Cover and cook on LOW for 3 to 4 hours. At least 1 hour before serving, remove chicken and cut into bite-size pieces.

- Combine cornstarch and soy sauce in bowl and mix well. Stir into slow cooker. Add onions, celery, bell pepper, mixed vegetables and molasses. Cover and cook on HIGH heat for 1 to 2 hours.

- Serve over chow mein noodles. Serves 4 to 6.

Chicken and Pasta

1 (16 ounce) package
   frozen whole green
   beans, thawed   455 g
1 onion, chopped
1 cup fresh mushroom
   halves   70 g
3 boneless, skinless
   chicken breast halves
1 (15 ounce) can Italian
   stewed tomatoes   425 g
1 teaspoon chicken
   bouillon granules   5 ml
1 teaspoon minced garlic   5 ml
1 teaspoon Italian
   seasoning   5 ml
1 (8 ounce) package
   fettuccini   230 g
1 (4 ounce) package
   grated parmesan
   cheese   115 g

- Place green beans, onion and mushrooms in sprayed 4-quart (4 L) slow cooker.

- Cut chicken into 1-inch (2.5 cm) pieces and place over vegetables.

- Combine stewed tomatoes, chicken bouillon, garlic and Italian seasoning in small bowl. Pour over chicken.

- Cover and cook on LOW for 5 to 6 hours.

- Cook fettuccini according to package directions and drain.

- Serve chicken over fettuccini sprinkled with parmesan cheese. Serves 4.

TIP: *Add ¼ cup (60 g) butter to make this dish have a richer taste.*

Chicken and Vegetables

4 - 5 boneless, skinless chicken breast halves

2 teaspoons seasoned salt   10 ml

1 (16 ounce) package frozen broccoli, cauliflower and carrots, thawed   455 g

1 (10 ounce) can cream of celery soup   280 g

1 (8 ounce) package shredded cheddar-Jack cheese, divided   230 g

- Cut chicken into strips, sprinkle with seasoned salt and place in sprayed slow cooker.

- Combine vegetables, celery soup and half cheese in large bowl and mix well. Spoon over chicken breasts.

- Cover and cook on LOW for 4 to 5 hours.

- About 10 minutes before serving, sprinkle remaining cheese on top of casserole. Serves 4 to 6.

Chicken Delicious

**5 - 6 boneless skinless
chicken breast halves**
**1 (16 ounce) package
frozen broccoli florets,
thawed   455 g**
**1 red bell pepper, seeded,
julienned**
**1 (16 ounce) jar parmesan-
mozzarella cheese
creation sauce   455 g**
3 tablespoons sherry   45 ml
Noodles, cooked

- Brown chicken breasts in skillet and place in sprayed, 5 to 6-quart (5 to 6 L) oval slow cooker.

- Place broccoli florets on plate, remove much of stem and discard.

- Combine broccoli florets, bell pepper, cheese sauce and sherry in bowl and mix well. Spoon over chicken breasts.

- Cover and cook on LOW for 4 to 5 hours. Serve over noodles. Serves 4 to 6.

Chicken Delight

¾ cup white rice	150 g
1 (14 ounce) can chicken broth	400 g
1 (1 ounce) packet onion soup mix	30 g
1 red bell pepper, seeded, chopped	
2 (10 ounce) cans cream of celery soup	2 (280 g)
¾ cup white cooking wine	175 ml
4 - 6 boneless skinless chicken breast halves	
1 (3 ounce) package grated fresh parmesan cheese	85 g

- Combine rice, broth, soup mix, bell pepper, celery soup, ¾ cup (175 ml) water, wine and several sprinkles of black pepper in bowl and mix well. (Make sure to mix soup well with liquids.)

- Place chicken breasts in sprayed 6-quart (6 L) oval slow cooker.

- Pour rice-soup mixture over chicken breasts.

- Cover and cook on LOW for 4 to 6 hours.

- One hour before serving, sprinkle parmesan cheese over chicken. Serves 4 to 6.

Chicken Dinner

1 cup rice	200 g
1 tablespoon chicken seasoning	15 ml
1 (1 ounce) packet onion soup mix	30 g
1 green bell pepper, seeded, chopped	
1 (4 ounce) jar diced pimentos, drained	115 g
¾ teaspoon dried basil	4 ml
1 (14 ounce) can chicken broth	400 g
1 (10 ounce) can cream of chicken soup	280 g
5 - 6 boneless, skinless chicken breast halves	

- Combine rice, chicken seasoning, onion soup mix, bell pepper, pimentos, basil, broth, ½ cup (125 ml) water and chicken soup in bowl and mix well.

- Place chicken breasts in sprayed, oval slow cooker and cover with rice mixture.

- Cover and cook on LOW for 6 to 7 hours. Serves 4 to 6.

Chicken-Supper Ready

6 medium new potatoes with peels, quartered	
4 - 5 carrots	
4 - 5 boneless, skinless chicken breast halves	
1 tablespoon chicken seasoning	15 ml
2 (10 ounce) cans cream of chicken soup	2 (280 g)
⅓ cup white wine or cooking wine	75 ml

- Cut carrots into ½-inch (1.2 cm) pieces. Place potatoes and carrots in slow cooker.

- Sprinkle chicken breasts with chicken seasoning and place over vegetables.

- Heat soups, wine and ¼ cup (60 ml) water in saucepan just to mix and pour over chicken and vegetables.

- Cover and cook on LOW for 5 to 6 hours. Serves 4 to 5.

Chicken Fajitas

2 pounds boneless,
   skinless chicken breast
   halves   **910 g**
1 onion, thinly sliced
1 red bell pepper, cored,
   seeded, julienned
1 teaspoon ground
   cumin   **5 ml**
1½ teaspoons chili
   powder   **7 ml**
1 tablespoon lime juice **15 ml**
½ cup chicken broth   **125 ml**
8 - 10 warm flour
   tortillas
Guacamole
Sour cream
Lettuce and tomatoes

- Cut chicken into diagonal strips and place in sprayed slow cooker. Top with onion and bell pepper.

- Combine cumin, chili powder, lime juice and chicken broth in bowl and pour over chicken and vegetables.

- Cover and cook on LOW for 5 to 7 hours.

- Serve several slices of chicken mixture with sauce into center of each warm tortilla and fold.

- Serve with guacamole, sour cream, lettuce or tomatoes or plain. Serves 4 to 6.

Chicken for Supper

5 - 6 boneless, skinless
chicken breast halves
6 carrots, peeled, cut
in 1-inch length   6 (2.5 cm)
1 (15 ounce) can cut
green beans,
drained   425 g
1 (15 ounce) can
whole new
potatoes, drained   425 g
2 (10 ounce) cans
cream of
mushroom soup   2 (280 g)
Shredded cheddar cheese

• Wash, dry chicken breasts
with paper towels and place in
sprayed, oval slow cooker.

• In bowl, combine, carrots, green
beans, potatoes and mushroom
soup and pour over chicken
in cooker.

• Cover and cook on LOW for
8 to 10 hours.

• When ready to serve, sprinkle
cheese over top. Serves 4 to 6.

Chicken-Ready Supper

1 (6 ounce) package
stuffing mix   170 g
3 cups cooked,
chopped chicken
breasts   420 g
1 (16 ounce) package
frozen whole green
beans, thawed   455 g
2 (12 ounce) jars
chicken gravy   2 (340 g)

• Prepare stuffing mix according
to package directions and place
in oval slow cooker.

• Follow with layer of chopped
chicken and place green beans
over chicken. Pour chicken
gravy over green beans.

• Cover and cook on LOW for
3 hours 30 minutes to 4 hours.
Serves 4 to 6.

Chicken Marseilles

4 - 5 boneless, skinless
    chicken breast
    halves
2 tablespoons butter   30 g
1 (2 ounce) packet
    leek soup and dip
    mix   60 g
½ teaspoon dill weed   2 ml
1 cup milk   250 ml
Brown rice, cooked
¾ cup sour cream   180 g

- Place chicken breasts in large, sprayed slow cooker.

- Combine butter, leek soup mix, dill weed, milk and ½ cup (125 ml) water in saucepan and heat just enough for butter to melt and ingredients to mix well. Pour over chicken.

- Cover and cook on LOW for 3 to 5 hours.

- When ready to serve, remove chicken breasts to platter with hot, cooked brown rice and cover to keep warm.

- Add sour cream to cooker liquid and stir well. Pour sauce over chicken and rice. Serves 4 to 5.

Chicken Breast Deluxe

4 slices bacon
5 - 6 boneless, skinless
   chicken breast
   halves
1 cup sliced celery   100 g
1 cup sliced red bell
   pepper   90 g
1 (10 ounce) can
   cream of chicken
   soup   280 g
2 tablespoons white
   wine or cooking
   wine   30 ml
6 slices Swiss cheese
2 tablespoons dried
   parsley   30 ml

- Cook bacon in large skillet, drain, crumble and reserve drippings. Place chicken in skillet with bacon drippings and lightly brown on both sides.

- Transfer chicken to sprayed, oval slow cooker and place celery and bell pepper over chicken.

- In same skillet, combine soup and wine, stir and spoon over vegetables and chicken. Cover and cook on LOW for 3 to 4 hours.

- Top with slices of cheese over each chicken breast and add parsley. Cook for additional 10 minutes.

- Serve with creamy sauce and sprinkle with crumbled bacon. Serves 4 to 6.

Chicken Supper

**5 boneless, skinless chicken
  breast halves**
**1 (16 ounce) jar alfredo
  sauce   455 g**
**1 (16 ounce) package
  frozen green peas,
  thawed   455 g**
**1½ cups shredded
  mozzarella cheese   170 g**
Noodles, cooked

- Cut chicken into strips and place in sprayed slow cooker.

- Combine alfredo sauce, peas and cheese in bowl and mix well. Spoon over chicken strips.

- Cover and cook on LOW for 5 to 6 hours.

- When ready to serve, spoon over noodles. Serves 4 to 5.

*TIP: If you want chicken supper
       in 1 casserole, cook
       1 (8 ounce/230 g) package
       noodles and mix with chicken
       and peas. Sprinkle a little
       extra cheese over top
       and serve.*

*TIP: Use 1 (10 ounce/280 g) can
       chicken soup and
       1 (10 ounce/280 g) can
       mushroom soup for a
       tasty change.*

Chow Mein Chicken

4 boneless, skinless
   chicken breast
   halves
2 - 3 cups sliced
   celery   200 - 300 g
1 onion, coarsely
   chopped
⅓ cup soy sauce   75 ml
¼ teaspoon cayenne
   pepper   1 ml
1 (14 ounce) can
   chicken broth   400 g
1 (15 ounce) can bean
   sprouts, drained   425 g
1 (8 ounce) can water
   chestnuts,
   drained   230 g
1 (6 ounce) can
   bamboo shoots   170 g
¼ cup flour   30 g
Chow mein noodles

- Combine chicken, celery, onion, soy sauce, cayenne pepper and chicken broth in sprayed slow cooker. Cover and cook on LOW for 3 to 4 hours.

- Add bean sprouts, water chestnuts and bamboo shoots to chicken. Mix flour and ¼ cup (60 ml) water in bowl and stir into chicken and vegetables.

- Cook for an additional 1 hour. Serve over chow mein noodles. Serves 4.

Classy Chicken Dinner

1 (6 ounce) box long
   grain-wild rice   170 g
1 (16 ounce) jar
   roasted
   garlic-parmesan
   cheese creation
   sauce   455 g
12 - 15 frozen chicken
   breast tenderloins,
   thawed
1 cup frozen petite
   green peas,
   thawed   145 g

- Pour 2½ cups (625 ml) water, rice and seasoning packet in sprayed 5-quart (5 L) slow cooker and stir well.

- Spoon in cheese creation and mix well. Place chicken tenderloins in slow cooker and cover with green peas.

- Cover and cook on LOW for 4 to 5 hours. Serves 4.

Creamy Chicken and Potatoes

4 boneless, skinless
   chicken breast halves
2 teaspoons chicken
   seasoning   10 ml
8 - 10 small new (red)
   potatoes with peels
1 (10 ounce) can cream of
   chicken soup   280 g
1 (8 ounce) carton sour
   cream   230 g

- Place chicken breast halves, sprinkled with chicken seasoning in slow cooker.

- Arrange new potatoes around chicken.

- Combine soup, sour cream and good amount of black pepper in bowl. Spoon over chicken breasts.

- Cover and cook on LOW for 4 to 6 hours. Serves 4.

Creamed Chicken

**4 large boneless, skinless
    chicken breast halves**
Lemon juice
**1 red bell pepper, seeded,
    chopped**
**2 ribs celery, sliced
    diagonally**
**1 (10 ounce) can cream
    of chicken soup   280 g**
**1 (10 ounce) can cream
    of celery soup   280 g**
⅓ cup dry white wine   75 ml
**1 (4 ounce) package
    grated parmesan
    cheese   115 g**
Rice, cooked

- Wash and pat chicken dry with paper towels, rub a little lemon juice over chicken and sprinkle with a little salt and pepper.

- Place in sprayed slow cooker and top with celery.

- Combine soups and wine in saucepan and heat just enough to mix thoroughly.

- Pour over chicken breasts and sprinkle with parmesan cheese.

- Cover and cook on LOW for 6 to 7 hours.

- Serve over rice. Serves 4 to 5.

Creamed Chicken and Vegetables

**4 large boneless, skinless
    chicken breast halves**
**1 (10 ounce) can cream of
    chicken soup**   **280 g**
**1 (16 ounce) package
    frozen peas and
    carrots, thawed**   **455 g**
**1 (12 ounce) jar chicken
    gravy**   **340 g**
**Buttermilk biscuits or
    Texas toast**

- Cut chicken in thin slices.

- Pour soup and ½ cup (125 ml) water into sprayed 6-quart (6 L) slow cooker, mix and add chicken slices.

- Sprinkle a little salt and lots of pepper over chicken and soup.

- Cover and cook on LOW for 4 to 5 hours.

- Add peas and carrots, chicken gravy and ½ cup (125 ml) water. Increase heat to HIGH and cook for about 1 hour or until peas and carrots are tender.

- Serve over large, refrigerated buttermilk biscuits or over Texas toast (thick slices of bread). Serves 4.

Creamy Salsa Chicken

4 - 5 boneless, skinless
   chicken breast halves
1 (1 ounce) packet dry
   taco seasoning mix   30 g
1 cup salsa   265 g
½ cup sour cream   120 g

- Place chicken breasts in sprayed 5 to 6-quart (5 to 6 L) slow cooker and add ¼ cup (60 ml) water.

- Sprinkle taco seasoning mix over chicken and top with salsa.

- Cover and cook on LOW for 5 to 6 hours.

- When ready to serve, remove chicken breasts and place on platter. Stir sour cream into salsa sauce and spoon over chicken breasts. Serves 4 to 5.

Delightful Chicken and Veggies

4 - 5 boneless, skinless
   chicken breast halves
1 (15 ounce) can whole
   kernel corn, drained   425 g
1 (10 ounce) box frozen
   green peas, thawed   280 g
1 (16 ounce) jar alfredo
   sauce   455 g
1 teaspoon chicken
   seasoning   5 ml
1 teaspoon minced garlic   5 ml
Pasta, cooked

- Brown chicken breasts in skillet and place in sprayed, oval slow cooker.

- Combine corn, peas, alfredo sauce, ¼ cup (60 ml) water, chicken seasoning and minced garlic in bowl and spoon mixture over chicken breasts.

- Cover and cook on LOW for 4 to 5 hours. Serve over pasta. Serves 4 to 5.

Slow Cooker Cordon Bleu

4 boneless, skinless chicken
    breast halves
4 slices cooked ham
4 slices Swiss cheese,
    softened
1 (10 ounce) can cream
    of chicken soup   **280 g**
¼ cup milk   **60 ml**
Noodles, cooked

- Place chicken breasts on cutting board and pound until breast halves are thin.

- Place ham and cheese slices on chicken breasts, roll and secure with toothpick.

- Arrange chicken rolls in sprayed 4-quart (4 L) slow cooker.

- Pour chicken soup with milk into saucepan, heat just enough to mix well and pour over chicken rolls.

- Cover and cook on LOW for 4 to 5 hours.

- Serve over noodles and cover with sauce from soup. Serves 4.

Delicious Chicken Pasta

1 pound chicken tenders	455 g
Lemon-herb chicken seasoning	
3 tablespoons butter	40 g
1 onion, coarsely chopped	
1 (15 ounce) can diced tomatoes	425 g
1 (10 ounce) can golden mushroom soup	280 g
1 (8 ounce) box angel hair pasta	230 g

- Pat chicken tenders dry with several paper towels and sprinkle ample amount of chicken seasoning.

- Melt butter in large skillet, brown chicken and place in oval slow cooker. Pour remaining butter and seasonings over chicken and cover with onion.

- In separate bowl, combine tomatoes and mushroom soup and pour over chicken and onions. Cover and cook on LOW for 4 to 5 hours.

- When ready to serve, cook pasta according to package directions. Serve chicken and sauce over pasta. Serves 4.

Farmhouse Supper

1 (8 ounce) package
   medium noodles   230 g
4 - 5 boneless, skinless
   chicken breast halves
Canola oil
1 (14 ounce) can chicken
   broth   400 g
2 cups sliced celery   200 g
2 onions, chopped
1 green bell pepper,
   seeded, chopped
1 red bell pepper, seeded,
   chopped
1 (10 ounce) can cream
   of chicken soup   280 g
1 (10 ounce) can cream
   of mushroom soup 280 g
1 cup shredded 4-cheese
   blend   115 g

- Cook noodles in boiling water until barely tender and drain well.

- Cut chicken into thin slices and brown lightly in skillet with a little oil

- Mix noodles, chicken and broth in large, sprayed slow cooker.

- Make sure noodles separate and coat with broth. Stir in remaining ingredients.

- Cover and cook on LOW for 4 to 6 hours. Serves 4 to 5.

Golden Chicken Dinner

**5 boneless, skinless
  chicken breast halves**
**6 medium new (red)
  potatoes with peels,
  cubed**
**6 medium carrots,
  chopped**
**1 tablespoon dried
  parsley flakes**   15 ml
1 teaspoon seasoned salt   5 ml
**1 (10 ounce) can golden
  mushroom soup**   280 g
**1 (10 ounce) can cream
  of chicken soup**   280 g
**4 tablespoons dried
  mashed potato flakes**   15 g
Water or milk

- Cut chicken into ½-inch (1.2 cm) pieces.

- Place potatoes and carrots in slow cooker and top with chicken breasts.

- Sprinkle parsley flakes, seasoned salt and ½ teaspoon (2 ml) pepper over chicken. Combine soups in bowl and spread over chicken.

- Cover and cook on LOW for 6 to 7 hours.

- Stir in potato flakes and a little water or milk if necessary to make gravy and cook for an additional 30 minutes.
  Serves 4 to 6.

Hawaiian Chicken

6 boneless, skinless chicken
   breast halves
1 (15 ounce) can pineapple
   slices with juice   425 g
⅓ cup packed brown
   sugar   75 g
2 tablespoons lemon juice 30 ml
¼ teaspoon ground ginger 1 ml
¼ cup cornstarch   30 g
Rice, cooked

- Place chicken breasts in sprayed, oval slow cooker and sprinkle with a little salt. Place pineapple slices over chicken.

- Combine pineapple juice, brown sugar, lemon juice, ginger and cornstarch in small bowl and stir until cornstarch mixes with liquids. Pour over chicken breasts.

- Cover and cook on LOW for 4 to 5 hours or on HIGH for 2 hours 30 minutes to 3 hours. Serve over rice. Serves 4 to 6.

Imperial Chicken

1 (6 ounce) box long
   grain-wild rice   170 g
1 (16 ounce) jar roasted
   garlic-parmesan cheese
   creation sauce   455 g
6 boneless, skinless
   chicken breast halves
1 (16 ounce) box frozen
   French-style green
   beans, thawed   455 g
½ cup slivered almonds,
   toasted   85 g

- Combine 2½ cups (625 ml) water, rice and seasoning packet into sprayed, oval slow cooker and stir well.

- Spoon in cheese creation and mix well. Place chicken breasts in slow cooker and cover with green beans.

- Cover and cook on LOW for 3 to 5 hours. When ready to serve, sprinkle with slivered almonds. Serves 4 to 6.

Here's the Stuff

5 boneless, skinless chicken breast halves

2 (10 ounce) cans cream of chicken soup   **2 (280 g)**

1 (6 ounce) box chicken stuffing mix   **170 g**

1 (16 ounce) package frozen green peas, thawed   **455 g**

- Place chicken breasts in 6-quart (6 L) slow cooker and spoon soups over chicken.

- Combine stuffing mix with ingredients on package directions, include seasoning packet in bowl and spoon over chicken and soup.

- Cover and cook on LOW for 5 to 6 hours.

- Sprinkle drained green peas over top of stuffing. Cover and cook for an additional 45 to 50 minutes. Serves 4 to 5.

TIP: Use 1 (10 ounce/280 g) can cream of chicken soup and 1 (10 ounce/280 g) can fiesta nacho soup for a nice variation.

Mushroom Chicken

4 boneless, skinless
  chicken breasts
  halves
1 (15 ounce) can
  tomato sauce   425 g
2 (4 ounce) cans
  sliced mushrooms,
  drained   2 (115 g)
1 (10 ounce) package
  frozen seasoning
  blend onions and
  peppers   280 g
2 teaspoons Italian
  seasoning   10 ml
1 teaspoon minced
  garlic   5 ml

- Brown chicken breasts in skillet and place in oval slow cooker.

- Combine tomato sauce, mushrooms, onions and peppers, Italian seasoning, garlic and ¼ cup (60 ml) water in bowl and spoon over chicken breasts.

- Cover and cook on LOW for 4 to 5 hours. Serves 4.

Orange Chicken

6 boneless, skinless
    chicken breast halves
1 (12 ounce) jar
    orange marmalade   340 g
1 (8 ounce) bottle Russian
    salad
    dressing   230 g
1 (1 ounce) packet
    onion soup mix   30 g

- Place chicken breasts in oval slow cooker. Combine orange marmalade, dressing, soup mix and ¾ cup (175 ml) water in bowl and stir well.

- Spoon mixture over chicken breasts. Cover and cook on LOW for 4 to 6 hours. Serves 4 to 6.

Oregano Chicken

½ cup (1 stick) butter,
    melted   115 g
1 (1 ounce) packet
    Italian salad dressing   30 g
1 tablespoon lemon juice   15 ml
4 - 5 boneless, skinless
    chicken breast halves
2 tablespoons dried
    oregano   30 ml

- Combine butter, dressing and lemon juice in bowl and mix well.

- Place chicken breasts in large, sprayed slow cooker. Spoon butter-lemon juice mixture over chicken.

- Cover and cook on LOW for 5 to 6 hours.

- One hour before serving, baste chicken with pan juices and sprinkle oregano over chicken. Serves 4 to 6.

Quick-Fix Chicken

4 - 6 boneless, skinless
   chicken breast halves
1 (8 ounce) carton
   sour cream   230 g
¼ cup soy sauce   60 ml
2 (10 ounce) cans
   French onion
   soup   2 (280 g)

- Wash and dry chicken with paper towels and place in sprayed, oval slow cooker.

- Combine sour cream, soy sauce and onion soup in bowl, stir and mix well. Add to slow cooker

- Cover and cook on LOW for 5 to 6 hours if chicken breasts are large, 3 to 4 hours if breasts are medium. Serves 4 to 6.

TIP: *Serve chicken and sauce with hot, buttered rice or mashed potatoes.*

Picante Chicken

4 boneless, skinless
   chicken breast halves
1 green bell pepper,
   seeded, cut in rings
1 (16 ounce) jar picante
   sauce   455 g
⅓ cup packed brown
   sugar   75 g
1 tablespoon mustard   15 ml

- Place chicken breasts in slow cooker with bell pepper rings over top of chicken.

- Combine picante, brown sugar and mustard in bowl and spoon over top of chicken.

- Cover and cook on LOW for 4 to 5 hours. Serves 4.

Perfect Chicken Breasts

1 (2.5 ounce) jar
   dried beef   70 g
6 small boneless,
   skinless chicken
   breast halves
6 slices bacon
2 (10 ounce) cans
   golden mushroom
   soup   2 (280 g)

- Line bottom of oval slow cooker with slices of dried beef and overlap some.

- Roll each chicken breast with slice of bacon and secure with toothpick. Place in slow cooker, overlapping as little as possible.

- Combine mushroom soup and ½ cup (125 ml) water or milk in bowl and spoon over chicken breasts.

- Cover and cook on LOW for 6 to 8 hours. Serves 4 to 6.

TIP: *When cooked, you will have a great "gravy" that is wonderful served over noodles or rice.*

Russian Chicken

1 (8 ounce) bottle Russian
   salad dressing   230 g
1 (16 ounce) can whole
   cranberry sauce   455 g
1 (1 ounce) packet onion
   soup mix   30 g
4 chicken quarters,
   skinned
Rice, cooked

- Combine salad dressing, cranberry sauce, ½ cup (125 ml) water and soup mix in bowl. Stir well to get all lumps out of soup mix.

- Place 4 chicken pieces in sprayed, 6-quart (6 L) oval slow cooker and spoon dressing-cranberry mixture over chicken.

- Cover and cook on LOW for 4 to 5 hours. Serve sauce and chicken over rice. Serves 4 to 6.

TIP: Use 6 chicken breasts if you don't want to cut up a chicken.

So-Good Chicken

4 - 5 boneless, skinless
   chicken breast halves
1 (10 ounce) can golden
   mushroom soup   280 g
1 cup white cooking
   wine   250 ml
1 (8 ounce) carton sour
   cream   230 g

- Wash, dry chicken breasts with paper towels and sprinkle a little salt and pepper over each.

- Combine mushroom soup, wine and sour cream in bowl and mix well. Spoon over chicken breasts.

- Cover and cook on LOW for 5 to 7 hours. Serves 4 to 6.

Winter Dinner

1 pound chicken
   tenderloins   455 g
Canola oil
1 pound Polish sausage,
   cut in 1-inch
   pieces   455 g/2.5 cm
2 onions, chopped
1 (28 ounce) can pork
   and beans with liquid   795 g
1 (15 ounce) can
   ranch-style beans,
   drained   425 g
1 (15 ounce) can great
   northern beans   425 g
1 (15 ounce) can butter
   beans, drained   425 g
1 cup ketchup   270 g
1 cup packed brown
   sugar   220 g
1 tablespoon
   vinegar   15 ml
6 slices bacon,
   cooked, crumbled

- Brown chicken slices in a little oil in skillet and place in large, sprayed slow cooker. Add sausage, onions, 4 cans beans, ketchup, brown sugar and vinegar and stir gently.

- Cover and cook on LOW for 7 to 8 hours or on HIGH for 3 hours 30 minutes to 4 hours.

- When ready to serve, sprinkle crumbled bacon over top. Serves 4 to 6.

Savory Chicken Fettuccini

2 pounds boneless, skinless chicken thighs, cubed	910 g
½ teaspoon garlic powder	2 ml
1 red bell pepper, seeded, chopped	
2 ribs celery, chopped	
1 (10 ounce) can cream of celery soup	280 g
1 (10 ounce) can cream of chicken soup	280 g
1 (8 ounce) package cubed Velveeta® cheese	230 g
1 (4 ounce) jar diced pimentos	115 g
1 (16 ounce) package spinach fettuccini	455 g

- Place cubed chicken pieces in slow cooker. Sprinkle with garlic powder, ½ teaspoon (2 ml) pepper, bell pepper and celery. Top with soups.

- Cover and cook on HIGH for 4 to 6 hours or until chicken juices are clear. Stir in cheese and pimentos. Cover and cook until cheese melts.

- Cook fettuccini according to package directions and drain. Place fettuccini in serving bowl and spoon chicken over fettuccini. Serve hot. Serves 4 to 6.

Scrumptious Chicken Breasts

There is a lot of delicious sauce.

**5 - 6 boneless, skinless
    chicken breast halves**
**1 teaspoon chicken
    seasoning   5 ml**
**1 (10 ounce) can cream
    of chicken soup   280 g**
**1 (10 ounce) can
    broccoli-cheese soup   280 g**
**½ cup white cooking
    wine   125 ml**
Noodles, cooked

- Place breast halves, sprinkled with black pepper and chicken seasoning, in sprayed oval slow cooker.

- Combine soups and wine in saucepan and heat enough to mix well. Pour over chicken.

- Cover and cook on LOW for 5 to 6 hours.

- Serve chicken and sauce over noodles. Serves 4 to 6.

TIP: If chicken breasts are very large, cut in half lengthwise. This is great served with roasted garlic, oven-baked Italian toast.

Smothered Chicken Breasts

4 boneless, skinless
   chicken breast
   halves
1 (10 ounce) can French
   onion soup   280 g
2 teaspoons chicken
   seasoning   10 ml
1 (4 ounce) jar sliced
   mushrooms, drained   115 g
1 cup shredded
   mozzarella cheese   115 g
Chopped green onions

- Brown each chicken breast in skillet and place in sprayed, oval slow cooker.

- Pour onion soup over chicken and sprinkle black pepper and chicken seasoning over chicken breasts.

- Place mushrooms and cheese over chicken breasts.

- Cover and cook on LOW for 4 to 5 hours. To give this chicken a really nice touch when ready to serve, sprinkle some chopped green onions over each serving. Serves 4.

Southwestern Chicken Pot

6 boneless, skinless
   chicken breast halves
1 teaspoon ground
   cumin   5 ml
1 teaspoon chili powder   5 ml
1 (10 ounce) can cream
   of chicken soup   280 g
1 (10 ounce) can fiesta
   nacho cheese soup   280 g
1 cup salsa   265 g
Rice, cooked
Flour tortillas

- Place chicken breasts sprinkled with cumin, chili powder and a little salt and pepper in sprayed, oval slow cooker.

- Combine soups and salsa in saucepan. Heat just enough to mix and pour over chicken breasts.

- Cover and cook on LOW for 6 to 7 hours. Serve over rice with warmed, flour tortillas spread with butter.
Serves 4 to 6.

Sweet-and-Sour Chicken

6 boneless, skinless
   chicken breast halves
Canola oil
1 (1 ounce) packet onion
   soup mix   30 g
1 (6 ounce) can frozen
   orange juice
   concentrate, thawed   170 g

- Brown chicken breasts in little oil in skillet and place in large, sprayed slow cooker.

- Combine onion soup mix, orange juice concentrate and ½ cup (125 ml) water in bowl and pour over chicken.

- Cover and cook on LOW for 3 to 5 hours. Serves 4 to 6.

Sunday Chicken

**4 large boneless, skinless
    chicken breast halves**
Chicken seasoning
4 slices American cheese
**1 (10 ounce) can cream
    of celery soup**   **280 g**
½ cup sour cream   **120 g**
**1 (6 ounce) box chicken
    stuffing mix**   **170 g**
**½ cup (1 stick) butter,
    melted**   **115 g**

- Wash and dry chicken breasts with paper towels and place in sprayed, oval slow cooker. Sprinkle each breast with chicken seasoning.

- Place slice of cheese over each chicken breast.

- Combine celery soup and sour cream in bowl, mix well and spoon over chicken and cheese.

- Sprinkle chicken stuffing mix over top of cheese. Drizzle melted butter over stuffing mix.

- Cover and cook on LOW for 5 to 6 hours. Serves 4.

Tasty Chicken-Rice and Veggies

4 boneless, skinless
   chicken breast halves
2 (10 ounce) jars
   sweet-and-sour
   sauce   2 (280 g)
1 (16 ounce) package
   frozen broccoli,
   cauliflower and
   carrots, thawed   455 g
1 (10 ounce) package
   frozen green peas,
   thawed   280 g
2 cups sliced celery   200 g
1 (6 ounce) package
   parmesan-butter
   rice mix   170 g
⅓ cup toasted,
   slivered almonds   55 g
Rice, cooked

- Cut chicken in 1-inch (2.5 cm) strips.

- Combine pieces, sweet-and-sour sauce and all vegetables in sprayed 6-quart (6 L) slow cooker.

- Cover and cook on LOW for 4 to 6 hours.

- When ready to serve, cook parmesan-butter rice according to package direction and fold in almonds.

- Serve chicken and vegetables over rice. Serves 4.

Honey-Baked Chicken

2 small fryer chickens,
   quartered
½ cup (1 stick) butter,
   melted   115 g
⅔ cup honey   230 g
¼ cup dijon-style
   mustard   60 g
1 teaspoon curry powder 5 ml

- Place chicken pieces in large slow cooker, skin-side up and sprinkle a little salt over chicken.

- Combine butter, honey, mustard and curry powder in bowl and mix well.

- Pour butter-mustard mixture over chicken quarters.

- Cover and cook on LOW for 6 to 8 hours. Baste chicken once during cooking. Serves 6 to 8.

Tangy Chicken

1 large fryer chicken,
   quartered
2 tablespoons butter   30 g
½ cup Heinz 57® sauce 125 ml
1 (15 ounce) can stewed
   tomatoes   425 g

- Wash, dry chicken quarters with paper towels and place in large slow cooker.

- Combine butter, 57 sauce and stewed tomatoes in saucepan. Heat just until butter melts and ingredients mix well. Pour over chicken.

- Cover and cook on LOW for 5 to 6 hours. Serves 4 to 6.

Chicken with Orange Sauce

1 whole chicken,
    quartered
½ cup plus 2 tablespoons
    flour   75 g
½ teaspoon ground
    nutmeg   2 ml
½ teaspoon ground
    cinnamon   2 ml
2 large sweet potatoes,
    peeled, sliced
1 (8 ounce) can pineapple
    chunks with juice   230 g
1 (10 ounce) can cream
    of chicken soup   280 g
⅔ cup orange juice   150 ml
Rice, cooked

- Wash and dry chicken quarters with paper towels. In bowl combine ½ cup (60 g) flour, nutmeg and cinnamon and coat chicken.

- Place sweet potatoes and pineapple in large, sprayed slow cooker. Arrange chicken on top.

- Combine chicken soup, orange juice and remaining flour in bowl and pour over chicken.

- Cover and cook on LOW for 7 to 9 hours or on HIGH for 3 to 4 hours. Serve over rice. Serves 4 to 6.

Tasty Chicken and Veggies

1 (2½ - 3 pound)
   whole chicken,
   quartered   1.1 - 1.4 kg
1 (16 ounce) package
   baby carrots   455 g
4 potatoes, peeled, sliced
3 ribs celery, sliced
1 onion, peeled, sliced
1 cup Italian salad
   dressing   250 ml
⅔ cup chicken broth   150 ml

- Rinse, dry and place chicken quarters in sprayed 6-quart (6 L) slow cooker with carrots, potatoes, celery and onion.

- Pour salad dressing and chicken broth over chicken and vegetables.

- Cover and cook on LOW for 6 to 8 hours. Serves 4 to 6.

TIP: When serving, garnish with sprigs of fresh parsley.

"Baked" Chicken

1 cup white rice   200 g
2 (10 ounce) cans
   cream of chicken
   soup   2 (280 g)
1 (14 ounce) can
   chicken broth   400 g
1 (1 ounce) packet
   onion soup mix   30 g
1 chicken, quartered

- Place rice in 5 to 6-quart (5 to 6 L) oval slow cooker.

- Combine chicken soup, broth, 2 soup cans water and onion soup mix in saucepan and mix well. Heat just enough to mix ingredients.

- Spoon half over rice and place 4 chicken quarters in slow cooker. Spoon remaining soup mixture over chicken.

- Cover and cook on LOW for 5 to 6 hours. Serves 4 to 6.

Saffron Rice and Chicken

1 fryer-broiler chicken,
   quartered
½ teaspoon garlic powder 2 ml
Canola oil
1 (14 ounce) can
   chicken broth   400 g
1 onion, chopped
1 green pepper, cored,
   seeded, quartered
1 yellow pepper, cored,
   seeded, quartered
1 (4 ounce) jar pimentos,
   drained   115 g
⅓ cup prepared
   bacon bits   20 g
2 tablespoons butter,
   melted   30 g
1 (5 ounce) package
   saffron yellow
   rice mix   145 g

- Sprinkle chicken with garlic powder and a little salt and pepper.

- Brown chicken quarters in little oil in skillet. Place chicken in sprayed, oval slow cooker and pour broth in slow cooker.

- Combine, onion, bell peppers, pimentos and bacon bits in bowl and spoon over chicken quarters.

- Cover and cook on LOW for 4 to 5 hours.

- Carefully remove chicken quarters from cooker in bowl, stir in butter and rice mix and return chicken to cooker.

- Cover and cook for additional 1 hour or until rice is tender. Serves 4 to 6.

Lemon Chicken

1 (2½ - 3 pound) chicken,	
quartered	1.1 - 1.4 kg
1 teaspoon dried oregano	5 ml
2 teaspoons minced garlic	10 ml
2 tablespoons butter	30 g
¼ cup lemon juice	60 ml

- Season chicken quarters with salt, pepper and oregano and rub garlic on chicken.

- Brown chicken quarters on all sides in butter in skillet and transfer to sprayed, oval slow cooker.

- Add ⅓ cup (75 ml) water to skillet, scrape bottom and pour over chicken.

- Cover and cook on LOW for 6 to 8 hours.

- At last hour of cooking, pour lemon juice over chicken, finish cooking. Serves 4 to 6.

Chicken Coq au Vin

**1 large fryer chicken,
  quartered, skinned**
Canola oil
**10 - 12 small white onions,
  peeled**
**½ pound whole
  mushrooms**   **230 g**
1 teaspoon minced garlic   **5 ml**
**½ teaspoon dried thyme
  leaves**   **2 ml**
**10 - 12 small new (red)
  potatoes with peels**
**1 (10 ounce) can chicken
  broth**   **280 g**
1 cup burgundy wine   **250 ml**
**6 bacon slices, cooked,
  crumbled**

- Brown chicken quarters in skillet on both sides and set aside.

- Place white onions, whole mushrooms, garlic and thyme in sprayed, oval slow cooker.

- Add chicken quarters, potatoes, chicken broth and a little salt and pepper.

- Cover and cook on LOW for 8 to 10 hours or on HIGH for 3 to 4 hours.

- During last hour, turn heat to HIGH, add wine and continue cooking.

- Sprinkle crumbled bacon over chicken before serving. Serves 4 to 6.

Chicken Cacciatore

2 onions, thinly sliced
1 (2½ - 3) pound fryer
   chicken,
   quartered   1.1 - 1.4 kg
2 (6 ounce) cans
   tomato paste   2 (170 g)
1 (4 ounce) can sliced
   mushrooms   115 g
1½ teaspoons minced
   garlic   7 ml
½ teaspoon dried
   basil   2 ml
2 teaspoons oregano
   leaves   10 ml
⅔ cup dry white
   wine   150 ml

- Place sliced onions in sprayed, oval slow cooker.

- Wash, dry chicken quarters with paper towels and place in slow cooker.

- Combine tomato paste, mushrooms, garlic, basil, oregano and wine in bowl and pour over chicken quarters.

- Cover and cook on LOW for 7 to 8 hours or on HIGH for 4 hours. Serves 4 to 6.

Taco Chicken

3 cups cooked,
    chopped chicken   420 g
1 (1 ounce) packet
    taco seasoning   30 g
1 cup white rice   200 g
2 cups chopped
    celery   200 g
1 green bell pepper,
    seeded, chopped
2 (15 ounce) cans
    Mexican stewed
    tomatoes   2 (425 g)

- Combine chicken, taco seasoning, rice, celery, bell pepper and stewed tomatoes in bowl and mix well.

- Pour into 5-quart (5 L) slow cooker. Cover and cook on LOW for 4 to 5 hours. Serves 4 to 6.

TIP: *This is a great recipe for leftover chicken.*

Tangy Chicken Legs

12 - 15 chicken legs
⅓ cup soy sauce   75 ml
⅔ cup packed brown
    sugar   150 g
Scant ⅛ teaspoon
    ground ginger   .5 ml

- Place chicken legs in sprayed 5-quart (5 L) slow cooker.

- Combine soy sauce, brown sugar, ¼ cup (60 ml) water and ginger in bowl and spoon over chicken legs.

- Cover and cook on LOW for 4 to 5 hours. Serves 6 to 8.

Monterey Bake

6 (6 inch) corn
    tortillas   6 (15 cm)
3 cups leftover cubed
    chicken   420 g
1 (10 ounce) package
    frozen whole
    kernel corn   280 g
1 (15 ounce) can pinto
    beans with liquid   425 g
1 (16 ounce) hot jar
    salsa   455 g
¼ cup sour cream   60 g
1 tablespoon flour   15 ml
3 tablespoons snipped
    fresh cilantro   5 g
1 (8 ounce) package
    shredded 4-cheese
    blend   230 g

- Preheat oven to 250° (120° C).

- Cut tortillas into 6 wedges. Place half of tortillas wedges in sprayed slow cooker.

- Place remaining wedges on baking pan, bake for about 10 minutes and set aside.

- Layer chicken, corn and beans over tortillas in cooker.

- Combine salsa, sour cream, flour and cilantro in bowl and pour over corn and beans.

- Cover and cook on LOW for 3 to 4 hours.

- When ready to serve, place baked tortillas wedges and cheese on top of each serving. Serves 4 to 6.

Chicken and Stuffing

1 (10 ounce) can cream
    of chicken soup   **280 g**
2 stalks celery, sliced
½ cup (1 stick) butter,
    melted   **115 g**
3 cups cooked, cubed
    chicken   **420 g**
1 (16 ounce) package
    frozen broccoli, corn
    and red peppers   **455 g**
1 (8 ounce) box cornbread
    stuffing mix   **230 g**

- Combine chicken soup, celery, butter, chicken, vegetables, stuffing mix and ⅓ cup (75 ml) water in large bowl.

- Mix well and transfer to 5 or 6-quart (5 to 6 L) slow cooker.

- Cover and cook on LOW for 5 to 6 hours. Serves 4 to 6.

TIP: This is a great recipe for leftover chicken.

Chicken and Everything Good

2 (10 ounce) cans cream of chicken soup	2 (280 g)
⅓ cup (⅔ stick) butter, melted	75 g
3 cups cooked, cubed chicken	420 g
1 (16 ounce) package frozen broccoli, corn and red peppers	455 g
1 (10 ounce) package frozen green peas	280 g
1 (8 ounce) package cornbread stuffing mix	230 g

- Combine soup, butter and ⅓ cup (75 ml) water in large bowl and mix well. Add chicken, vegetables and stuffing mix and stir well. Spoon mixture into large, sprayed slow cooker.

- Cover and cook on LOW for 5 to 6 hours or on HIGH for 2 hours 30 minutes to 3 hours. Serves 4 to 6.

Chicken Alfredo

1½ pounds boneless, skinless
chicken thighs, cut
into strips   680 g
2 ribs celery, sliced
diagonally
1 red bell pepper, cored,
seeded,
julienned
1 (16 ounce) jar
alfredo sauce   455 g
3 cups fresh broccoli
florets   215 g
1 (8 ounce) package
fettuccini or linguine   230 g
1 (4 ounce) package
grated parmesan
cheese   115 g

- Cut chicken into strips.
- Layer chicken, celery and bell pepper in sprayed 4 to 5-quart (4 to 5 L) slow cooker.
- Pour alfredo sauce evenly over vegetables.
- Cover and cook on LOW for 5 to 6 hours.
- About 30 minutes before serving, turn heat to HIGH and add broccoli florets to chicken-alfredo mixture.
- Cover and cook for an additional 30 minutes.
- Cook pasta according to package directions and drain.
- Just before serving pour pasta into cooker, mix and sprinkle parmesan cheese on top. Serves 4 to 6.

Sweet and Spicy Chicken

2 pounds chicken thighs	910 g
¾ cup chili sauce	205 g
¾ cup packed brown sugar	165 g
1 (1 ounce) packet dry onion soup mix	30 g
¼ teaspoon cayenne pepper	1 ml
Rice, cooked	

- Arrange chicken pieces in sprayed 5-quart (5 L) slow cooker.

- Combine chili sauce, brown sugar, dry onion soup mix, cayenne pepper and ¼ cup (60 ml) water in bowl and spoon over chicken.

- Cover and cook on LOW for 6 to 7 hours. Serve over rice. Serves 4 to 6.

Maple-Plum Glazed Turkey Breast

1 cup red plum jam	320 g
1 cup maple syrup	250 ml
1 teaspoon dry mustard	5 ml
¼ cup lemon juice	60 ml
1 (3 - 5 pound) boneless turkey breast	1.4 - 2.3 kg

- Combine jam, syrup, mustard and lemon juice in saucepan. Bring to a boil, turn heat down and simmer for about 20 minutes or until slightly thick. Reserve 1 cup (250 ml).

- Place turkey breast in slow cooker and pour remaining glaze over turkey.

- Cover and cook on LOW for 5 to 7 hours.

- When ready to serve, slice turkey and serve with heated, reserved glaze. Serves 6 to 8.

Southern Chicken

1 cup half-and-half cream	250 ml
1 tablespoon flour	15 ml
1 (1 ounce) packet chicken gravy mix	30 g
1 pound boneless, skinless chicken thighs	455 g
1 (16 ounce) package frozen stew vegetables, thawed	455 g
1 (4 ounce) jar sliced mushrooms, drained	115 g
1 (10 ounce) package frozen green peas, thawed	280 g
1½ cups biscuit baking mix	180 g
1 bunch fresh green onions, chopped	
½ cup milk	125 ml

- Combine cream, flour, gravy mix and 1 cup (250 ml) water in bowl, stir until smooth and pour in large slow cooker.

- Cut chicken into 1-inch (2.5 cm) pieces and stir in vegetables and mushrooms.

- Cover and cook on LOW for 4 to 6 hours or until chicken is tender and sauce thickens. Stir in peas.

- Combine baking mix, onions and milk in bowl and mix well.

- Drop tablespoonfuls of dough onto chicken mixture.

- Change heat to HIGH, cover and cook for an additional 50 to 60 minutes. Serves 4 to 6.

Italian Chicken

1 small head cabbage
1 onion
1 (4 ounce) jar sliced
    mushrooms,
    drained   115 g
1 medium zucchini,
    sliced
1 red bell pepper, cored,
    seeded, julienned
1 teaspoon Italian
    seasoning   5 ml
1½ pounds boneless,
    skinless chicken
    thighs   680 g
1 teaspoon minced
    garlic   5 ml
2 (15 ounce) cans
    Italian stewed
    tomatoes   2 (425 g)
Parmesan cheese

- Cut cabbage into wedges, slice onions and separate into rings.

- Make layers of cabbage, onion, mushrooms, zucchini and bell pepper in sprayed 6-quart (6 L) slow cooker.

- Sprinkle Italian seasoning over vegetables. Place chicken thighs on top of vegetables.

- Mix garlic with tomatoes in bowl and pour over chicken.

- Cover and cook on LOW for 4 to 6 hours. When serving, sprinkle a little parmesan cheese over each serving. Serves 4 to 6.

Asparagus-Cheese Chicken

8 - 10 boneless, skinless
   chicken thighs
2 tablespoons butter   30 g
1 (10 ounce) can cream
   of celery soup   280 g
1 (10 ounce) can cheddar
   cheese soup   280 g
⅓ cup milk   75 ml
1 (16 ounce) package
   frozen asparagus cuts   455 g

- Place chicken thighs in sprayed 5-quart (5 L) slow cooker.

- Combine butter, celery soup, cheddar cheese soup and milk in saucepan. Heat just enough for butter to melt and mix well. Pour over chicken thighs.

- Cover and cook on LOW for 5 to 6 hours.

- Remove cover and place asparagus cuts over chicken and cook for an additional 1 hour. Serves 4 to 6.

Cheesy Chicken and Noodles

1 (8 ounce) package wide noodles	230 g
1 (10 ounce) can cream of chicken soup	280 g
4 cups cooked, chopped chicken breast	560 g
1 (15 ounce) ricotta cheese, softened, cut in cubes	425 g
1 (8 ounce) package shredded mozzarella cheese	230 g
1 (16 ounce) package frozen chopped onions and bell peppers	455 g
2 ribs celery, sliced	
1 (10 ounce) can chicken broth	280 g
1 teaspoon white pepper	5 ml

- Cook noodles according to package directions and drain.

- Place noodles, soup, chicken, ricotta cheese, mozzarella cheese, onions and bell peppers, celery and broth in sprayed slow cooker; stir until ingredients blend well.

- Sprinkle white pepper over top of ingredients and cook on LOW for 7 to 9 hours or on HIGH for 3 hours 30 minutes. Serves 6.

Stupendous Rice and Chicken

2 (10 ounce) cans
   cream of chicken
   soup   2 (280 g)
2 (4 ounce) boxes
   long-wild rice   2 (115 g)
1 red bell pepper,
   seeded, cut into
   strips
1 green bell pepper,
   seeded, cut into
   strips
1 (4 ounce) can sliced
   mushrooms   115 g
4 - 5 boneless, skinless
   chicken breast halves

- Combine chicken soup, rice, seasoning packets and 2 cups (500 ml) water in large bowl. Pour half mixture into sprayed 4 to 5 quart (4 to 5 L) slow cooker (must be large slow cooker because rice will expand during cooking).

- Layer bell pepper strips, mushrooms and chicken breasts on top and pour remaining soup-rice mixture over chicken.

- Cover and cook on LOW for 6 to 7 hours or on HIGH for 3 to 4 hours. Do not cook any longer than above time as rice will become mushy if over cooked. Serves 4 to 5.

Three Hour Chicken

1 (10 ounce) can cream of chicken soup	280 g
1 (4 ounce) can sliced mushrooms	115 g
1 small onion, finely chopped	
1 teaspoon Italian seasoning	5 ml
1½ pounds skinless, boneless chicken breasts, cut in \strips	680 g
Rice, cooked	

- Combine soup, mushrooms, onion and seasonings in sprayed slow cooker. Add chicken strips.

- Cover and cook on LOW for 2 hours 30 minutes to 3 hours. Serve over rice. Serves 4.

Arroz con Pollo

3 pounds chicken thighs	
2 (15 ounce) cans Italian stewed tomatoes	2 (425 g)
1 (16 ounce) package frozen green peas, thawed	455 g
2 cups long grain rice	370 g
1 (.28 ounce) packet yellow rice seasoning mix	10 g
2 (14 ounce) cans chicken broth	2 (400 g)
1 heaping teaspoon minced garlic	5 ml

- 1 teaspoon dried oregano 5 ml

- Combine all ingredients plus ¾ cup (175 ml) water in large, sprayed slow cooker and stir well.

- Cover and cook on LOW for 7 to 8 hours or on HIGH for 3 hours 30 minutes to 4 hours. Serves 6 to 8.

Yes to This Chicken

5 - 6 boneless, skinless
   chicken breast halves
1 (8 ounce) bottle
   Italian-style
   salad dressing   230 g
1 (10 ounce) can
   chicken broth   280 g
1 (11 ounce) can
   Mexicorn®, drained   310 g
1 (8 ounce) package
   shredded Velveeta
   cheese   230 g
¾ teaspoon dried basil   4 ml
1 (12 ounce) package
   pasta   340 g

- Place chicken breasts in sprayed, oval slow cooker. Pour salad dressing over chicken; cover and cook on LOW for 6 to 8 hours.

- Drain juices from slow cooker and stir in broth, corn, cheese, basil and a little salt and pepper. Combine and cook on LOW for an additional 1 hour.

- Cook your favorite pasta, drain and place on serving platter. Place chicken over pasta and spoon mixture over chicken breasts. Serves 5 to 6.

Turkey Bake

1½ pounds turkey tenderloins	680 g
1 (6 ounce) package Oriental rice and vermicelli	170 g
1 (10 ounce) package frozen green peas, thawed	280 g
1 cup sliced celery	100 g
¼ cup (½ stick) butter, melted	60 g
1 (14 ounce) can chicken broth	400 g
1½ cups fresh broccoli florets	105 g

- Cut tenderloins into strips. Saute turkey strips in non-stick skillet until it is no longer pink.

- Combine turkey strips, rice-vermicelli mix plus seasoning packet, peas, celery, butter, chicken broth and 1 cup (250 ml) water in large slow cooker and mix well.

- Cover and cook on LOW for 4 to 5 hours. Turn heat to HIGH setting, add broccoli and cook for an additional 20 minutes. Serves 4 to 6.

Turkey Loaf

2 pounds ground turkey	**910 g**
1 onion, very finely chopped	
½ red bell pepper, very finely chopped	
2 teaspoons minced garlic	**10 ml**
½ cup chili sauce	**135 g**
2 large eggs, beaten	
¾ cup Italian seasoned breadcrumbs	**175 ml**

- Make foil handles by cutting 3 (3 x 18-inch/8 x 45 cm) strips of heavy foil; place in bottom of slow cooker in crisscross strips (resembles spokes on wheel) up and over sides.

- Combine all ingredients plus 1 teaspoon (5 ml) salt and ½ teaspoon (2 ml) pepper in large bowl and mix well.

- Shape into round loaf and place on top foil. Fold extended strips over food. When finished cooking, lift food out by handles.

- Cover and cook on LOW for 5 to 6 hours. Serves 4 to 6.

Turkey Spaghetti

2 pounds ground turkey	910 g
2 (10 ounce) cans tomato bisque soup	2 (280 g)
1 (14 ounce) can chicken broth	400 g
2 (7 ounce) boxes ready-cut spaghetti, cooked, drained	2 (200 g)
1 (15 ounce) can whole kernel corn, drained	425 g
1 (4 ounce) can sliced mushrooms, drained	115 g
¼ cup ketchup	70 g

- Cook ground turkey in non-stick skillet and season with a little salt and pepper. Place cooked turkey in 5 to 6-quart (5 to 6 L) slow cooker.

- Add in soup, broth, spaghetti, corn, mushrooms and ketchup and stir to blend.

- Cover and cook on LOW for 5 to 7 hours or on HIGH for 3 hours. Serves 4 to 6.

Turkey Cassoulet

2 cups cooked, cubed turkey	280 g
1 (8 ounce) package smoked turkey sausage	230 g
3 carrots, sliced	
1 onion, halved, sliced	
1 (15 ounce) can navy beans	425 g
1 (15 ounce) can white lima beans	425 g
1 (8 ounce) can tomato sauce	230 g
1 teaspoon dried thyme	5 ml
¼ teaspoon ground allspice	1 ml

- Cut turkey sausage in ½-inch (1.2 cm) pieces.

- Combine all ingredients in sprayed slow cooker.

- Cover and cook on LOW for 4 to 5 hours. Serves 4.

TIP: This is a great recipe for leftover turkey

Colorful Rice and Turkey

1 (10 ounce) can cream of mushroom	280 g
1 (10 ounce) can cream of chicken soup	280 g
2 cups white rice	200 g
3 ribs celery, sliced diagonally	
1 (16 ounce) package frozen Oriental vegetable mix	455 g
3 cups cooked, cubed turkey (or chicken)	420 g
1 teaspoon poultry seasoning	5 ml
2 (14 ounce) cans chicken broth	2 (400 g)

- Pour mushroom soup and chicken soup in saucepan and add 1 soup can water. Heat just enough to mix well and pour into sprayed 5 to 6-quart (5 to 6 L) slow cooker.

- Add remaining ingredients and mix.

- Cover and cook on LOW for 5 to 6 hours. Serves 4 to 6.

Sausage and Rice

1 pound turkey sausage	455 g
1 (6 ounce) box flavored rice mix	170 g
2 (14 ounce) cans chicken broth	2 (400 g)
2 cups sliced celery	200 g
1 red bell pepper, cored, seeded, julienned	
1 (15 ounce) can cut green beans, drained	425 g
⅓ cup slivered almonds, toasted	55 g

- Break up turkey sausage and brown in skillet.

- Place in sprayed 4 to 5-quart (4 to 5 L) slow cooker.

- Add rice, 1 cup (250 ml) water, chicken broth, celery, bell pepper and green beans and stir to mix.

- Cover and cook on LOW for 3 to 4 hours.

- When ready to serve, sprinkle almonds over top. Serves 4.

Pork & Seafood

Chops, Loins, Loaves & Hams

Pork & Seafood Contents

Pork

Stuffed Pork Chops 249
Good Time Chops, Tators and Peas . . .250
Smothered Pork Chop Dinner 251
Pork Chops Deluxe 252
Savory Pork Chops 253
Ranch Pork Chops 253
Pork Chops with Orange Sauce 254
Western Pork Supper 255
Pork Chops for Supper 256
Pork Chops and Gravy 257
Pork Chops Pizza 258
Promising Pork Chops 259
Pineapple-Pork Chops 260
Peachy Pork Chops 261
Italian Pork Chops 262
Honey-Mustard Pork Chops 263
"Baked" Pork Chops 264
Delicious Pork Chops 264
Country Pork Chops 265
Pork Roast with Apricot Glaze 266
Show Time Pork Roast 267
Fruit-Stuffed Pork Roast 268
Pork with a Cranberry Glaze 269
Tender Pork Loin 270
Terrific Pork Tenderloin 270
Spinach-Stuffed Pork Roast 271
Pork and Cabbage Supper 272
Roasted Red Pepper Tenderloin 273

Honey-Mustard Pork Roast 273
Ginger Pork 274
Barbecue Pork Roast 275
Tangy Apricot Ribs 276
Finger Lickin' Baby Backs 276
Delectable Apricot Ribs 277
Home-Style Ribs 277
Saucy Ham Loaf 278
Sweet-and-Hot Mustard 278
Walnut Ham 279
Sweet-and-Sour Sausage Links 279
Zesty Ham Supper 280
Apricot Ham 281
Ben's Ham and Rice 281
Ham Loaf 282
Special Ham Supper 283
Ham and Potato Dish 284
Creamy Potatoes and Ham 285
Creamed Ham with Spaghetti 285
Ham to the Rescue 286
Ham and Potato Casserole 287
Tortellini Italian-Style 288
Celebrated Sausage and Rice 289
Sausage and Beans 290
Sauerkraut and Bratwurst 291

Seafood

Tuna OK Bake 291
Cheddar Crab Casserole 292

Stuffed Pork Chops

4 - 5 (1 inch) thick
    pork chops   4 - 5 (2.5 cm)
1 (15 ounce) can
    mixed vegetables,
    well drained   425 g
1 (8 ounce) can whole
    kernel corn, drained   230 g
½ cup rice   200 g
1 cup Italian-seasoned
    breadcrumbs   120 g
1 (15 ounce) can stewed
    tomatoes, slightly
    drained   425 g

- Cut pocket in each pork chop and season with a little salt and pepper.

- Combine vegetables, corn, rice and breadcrumbs in large bowl and stuff pork chops with vegetable mixture. Secure open sides with toothpicks.

- Place remaining vegetable mixture in 5-quart (5 L) slow cooker. Add pork chops and spoon stewed tomatoes over top of pork chops.

- Cover and cook on LOW for 8 to 9 hours.

- Serve vegetable mixture along with pork chops. Serves 4 to 5.

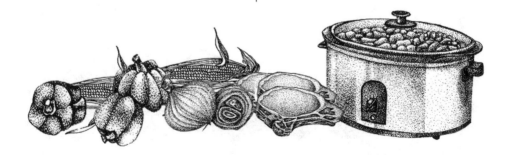

Good Time Chops, Tators and Peas

1 (10 ounce) can
   cream of
   mushrooms soup   280 g
1 (4 ounce) can sliced
   mushrooms   115 g
5 - 6 boneless pork
   chops
Lemon pepper
2 (15 ounce) cans
   whole new
   potatoes, drained   2 (425 g)
1 (10 ounce) can
   frozen green peas,
   thawed   280 g

- Spoon soup and mushrooms in sprayed slow cooker and stir in ¼ cup (60 ml) water to thin soup slightly.

- Season each pork chop with lemon pepper and place in slow cooker.

- Cover and cook on LOW for 6 to 8 hours.

- Remove lid and place potatoes and peas around pork chops; turn heat to HIGH and cook for an additional 1 hour 30 minutes. Serves 5.

Smothered Pork Chop Dinner

6 (¾ inch thick) bone-in pork chops	6 (1.8 cm)
8 - 10 medium red (new) potatoes with peels	
2 onions, sliced	
1 (10 ounce) can cream of chicken soup	280 g
1 (10 ounce) can chicken broth	280 g
¼ cup dijon-style mustard	60 g
1 teaspoon dried basil leaves	5 ml

- Brown pork chops sprinkled with a little salt and pepper in non-stick skillet. Place potatoes and onions in 5 to 6-quart (5 to 6 L) slow cooker and add browned pork chops.

- Combine soup, mustard and basil leaves in saucepan. Heat just enough to mix well and pour over pork chops. Cover and cook on LOW for 7 to 9 hours. Serves 4 to 6.

TIP: To "dress up" the pork chops, add 1 (3 ounce/85 g) can fried onion rings.

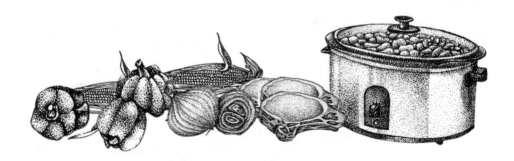

Pork Chops Deluxe

6 (1 inch thick)
   boneless pork
   chops   6 (2.5 cm)
1 teaspoon seasoned
   salt   5 ml
1 (11 ounce) can
   Mexicorn®,
   drained   310 g
1 (10 ounce) package
   frozen chopped
   onions and bell
   peppers, thawed 280 g
1 (4 ounce) can sliced
   mushrooms,
   drained, chopped 115 g
1¼ cups seasoned
   breadcrumbs   150 g
1 (8 ounce) can
   tomato
   sauce   230 g
1 (4 ounce) can
   green chilies   115 g

- Cut pocket in each pork chop, cutting from side almost to edge. Season pockets with the seasoned salt.

- In a bowl, combine Mexicorn®, onions and bell peppers, mushrooms, and breadcrumbs in bowl. Pack vegetable mixture into pockets and secure along open side with wooden picks.

- Spread any remaining vegetable mixture in sprayed slow cooker. Combine tomato sauce and green chilies in bowl and mix well.

- Moisten top surface of each stuffed chop with tomato mixture and place in slow cooker. Pour remaining tomato mixture on top of pork chops.

- Cover and cook on LOW for 8 to 9 hours or on HIGH for 4 to 5 hours. When ready to serve, remove pork chops to serving platter and mound vegetable mixture in center. Serves 6.

Savory Pork Chops

6 (¾ inch thick) pork chops	6 (1.8 cm)
1 cup pineapple juice	250 ml
⅓ cup packed brown sugar	75 g
3 tablespoons cider vinegar	45 ml
Noodles, cooked	

• Brown pork chops in skillet on both sides and place in 5-quart (5 L) slow cooker.

• Combine pineapple juice, brown sugar and vinegar in bowl and mix well.

• Pour brown sugar-vinegar mixture over pork chops.

• Cover and cook on LOW for 4 to 5 hours.

• Serve over noodles. Serves 4 to 6.

Ranch Pork Chops

6 (¾ inch thick) bone-in pork chops	6 (1.8 cm)
1 (.04 ounce) packet ranch dressing mix	10 g
2 (15 ounce) cans new potatoes, drained, quartered	2 (425 g)
1 (10 ounce) can French onion soup	280 g

• Place pork chops in sprayed 6-quart (6 L) oval slow cooker.

• Sprinkle pork chops with ranch dressing mix and ½ teaspoon (2 ml) pepper.

• Place potatoes around pork chops and pour French onion soup around potatoes and chops.

• Cover and cook on LOW for 4 to 5 hours. Serves 4 to 6.

Pork Chops with Orange Sauce

2 medium sliced yellow
    squash
2 onions, sliced
6 - 8 bone-in pork chops
½ cup chicken broth   125 ml
½ cup orange marmalade 160 g
1 tablespoon
    honey-mustard   15 ml
2 tablespoons cornstarch 15 g

- Place squash and onions in
  5 to 6-quart (5 to 6 L)
  slow cooker.

- Sprinkle a little salt and pepper
  on top of pork chops and place
  over vegetables.

- Combine broth, marmalade and
  mustard in bowl and spoon over
  pork chops.

- Cover and cook on LOW for
  4 to 6 hours.

- Transfer pork chops and
  vegetables to serving plate and
  cover to keep warm.

- For sauce, pour liquid from slow
  cooker into medium saucepan.
  Combine 2 tablespoons (30 ml)
  water with cornstarch and add
  to saucepan.

- Heat mixture, stir constantly
  until thick and serve over pork
  chops and vegetables.
  Serves 6 to 8.

Western Pork Supper

6 (¾ inch thick) boneless pork chops	6 (1.8 cm)
1 (15 ounce) can chili beans	425 g
1½ cups salsa	395 g
1 (16 ounce) package frozen seasoned corn with black beans, tomatoes, bell peppers, onions, thawed	455 g
1 (4 ounce) can sliced ripe olives	115 g
1½ - 2 cups instant brown rice	145 - 190 g
2 tablespoons butter, melted	30 g

- Arrange pork chops in sprayed, oval slow cooker and cover with chili beans and salsa.

- Cover and cook on LOW for 5 hours or on HIGH for 2 hours 30 minutes.

- Increase heat to HIGH (if cooking on LOW) and stir in seasoned corn. Cover and cook for an additional 30 minutes.

- Cook brown rice according to package directions and stir in melted butter.

- Place on serving platter. Spoon pork chops and vegetables over rice. Serves 6.

Pork Chops for Supper

6 (¾ inch thick) pork
   loin chops   6 (1.8 cm)
1 onion, halved, sliced
1 (8 ounce) can
   tomato sauce   230 g
¼ cup packed brown
   sugar   55 g
1 tablespoon
   Worcestershire
   sauce   15 ml
1 teaspoon seasoned
   salt   5 ml

- Brown pork chops in skillet on both sides and place in 4 to 5-quart (4 to 5 L) slow cooker. Place onions over pork chops.

- Combine tomato sauce, brown sugar, Worcestershire sauce, seasoned salt and ¼ cup (60 ml) water in bowl and spoon over onions and pork chops.

- Cover and cook on LOW for 4 to 5 hours. Serves 4 to 6.

Pork Chops and Gravy

6 (½ inch thick) pork
chops   6 (1.2 cm)
8 - 10 new (red)
potatoes with peels,
quartered
1 (16 ounce) package
baby carrots   455 g
2 (10 ounce) cans
cream of mushroom
soup with roasted
garlic   2 (280 g)

- Sprinkle a little salt and pepper on pork chops.

- Brown pork chops in skillet and place in 5 to 6-quart (5 to 6 L) slow cooker. Place potatoes and carrots around pork chops.

- Heat mushroom soup with ½ cup (125 ml) water in saucepan and pour over chops and vegetables.

- Cover and cook on LOW for 6 to 7 hours. Serves 4 to 6.

Pork Chops Pizza

6 (1 inch) thick
   boneless pork
   chops   6 (2.5 cm)
1 onion, finely chopped
1 green bell pepper,
   seeded, finely
   chopped
1 (8 ounce) jar pizza
   sauce   230 g
1 (10 ounce) box plain
   couscous   280 g
2 tablespoons butter   30 g
1 cup shredded
   mozzarella cheese 115 g

- Trim fat from pork chops and sprinkle with a little salt and pepper. Brown and cook pork chops in skillet on both sides for 5 minutes.

- Transfer chops to sprayed, oval slow cooker. Spoon onion and bell pepper over chops and pour pizza sauce over top.

- Cover and cook on LOW for 4 to 6 hours. Cook couscous according to package directions except add 2 tablespoons (28 g) butter instead of 1 tablespoon (15 ml) and place on serving platter.

- Spoon chops and sauce over couscous and sprinkle cheese over chops. Serves 4 to 6.

Promising Pork Chops

6 boneless pork chops
1 (4 ounce) can sliced
    mushrooms   **115 g**
1 (7 ounce) can tomatoes
    and green chilies   **200 g**
1 (10 ounce) can cream
    of mushroom soup   **280 g**
1 (8 ounce) carton sour
    cream   **230 g**
1 (8 ounce) package
    penne pasta   **230 g**

- Place pork chops in sprayed 5-quart (5 L) slow cooker and layer mushrooms, tomatoes and green chilies over top. Spread mushroom soup with large spoon over top.

- Cover and cook on LOW for 6 to 8 hours. Transfer pork chops to container that can be kept warm in oven.

- Stir sour cream into sauce in slow cooker and cook on HIGH for about 10 minutes.

- Cook pasta according to package directions.

- Stir pasta into sauce and place pork chops on top. Or if you prefer, place pasta-sauce on serving platter and top with warm pork chops. Serves 6.

Pineapple-Pork Chops

6 - 8 (½ inch thick)
   boneless pork
   chops   6 - 8 (1.2 cm)
Canola oil
1 (6 ounce) can
   frozen pineapple
   juice concentrate,
   thawed   170 g
¼ cup packed brown
   sugar   55 g
⅓ cup wine or tarragon
   vinegar   75 ml
⅓ cup honey   115 g
1 (6 ounce) package
   parmesan-butter
   rice, cooked   170 g

- Brown pork chops in a little oil in skillet and transfer to sprayed slow cooker.

- Combine pineapple juice concentrate, brown sugar, vinegar and honey in bowl. Pour over pork chops.

- Cover and cook on LOW for 5 to 6 hours. Serve over rice. Serves 6 to 8.

Peachy Pork Chops

6 - 8 (¾ inch thick)
   bone-in pork
   chops   6 - 8 (1.8 cm)
½ cup packed
   brown sugar   110 g
¼ teaspoon ground
   cinnamon   1 ml
¼ teaspoon ground cloves 1 ml
1 (8 ounce) can tomato
   sauce   230 g
1 (28 ounce) can peach
   halves with juice   795 g
¼ cup white vinegar   60 ml

- Brown pork chops in skillet on both sides and place in oval slow cooker.

- Combine brown sugar, cinnamon, cloves, tomato sauce, ¼ cup (60 ml) juice from peaches and vinegar in bowl.

- Pour sugar-tomato sauce mixture over pork chops and place peach halves over top. Cover and cook on LOW for 4 to 5 hours. Serves 6 to 8.

Italian Pork Chops

6 - 8 (1 inch) thick
  boneless pork
  chops   6 - 8 (2.5 cm)
½ pound fresh
  mushrooms, sliced   230 g
1 (10 ounce) package
  frozen onion-bell
  pepper blend, thawed   280 g
1 teaspoon Italian
  seasoning   5 ml
1 (15 ounce) can Italian
  stewed
  tomatoes   425 g

- Brown pork chops in skillet and sprinkle with salt and pepper on both sides.

- Combine mushrooms, onion-bell pepper blend and Italian seasoning in 6-quart (6 L) slow cooker and set aside.

- Place pork chops over vegetables and pour stewed tomatoes over pork chops. Cover and cook on LOW for 7 to 8 hours. To serve, spoon mushroom-seasoning blend over pork chops. Serves 6 to 8.

Honey-Mustard Pork Chops

Try this sauce over hot, cooked rice. It is wonderful!

1 (10 ounce) can golden
    mushroom soup   280 g
⅓ cup white wine   75 ml
¼ cup honey-mustard   60 g
1 teaspoon minced garlic 5 ml
4 - 5 (¾ inch thick)
    pork chops   4 - 5 (1.8 cm)

- Combine soup, wine, honey-mustard, minced garlic and 1 teaspoon (5 ml) salt in large bowl and mix well.

- Place pork chops, sprinkled with a little black pepper in 5-quart (5 L) slow cooker and spoon soup-honey-mustard mixture over chops.

- Cover and cook on LOW for 5 to 6 hours.

- When ready to serve, lift pork chops out of sauce and onto serving plate. Stir sauce to mix well and serve with chops. Serves 4 to 5.

TIP: For a "meat and potato meal", just slice 3 potatoes and place in slow cooker before adding pork chops.

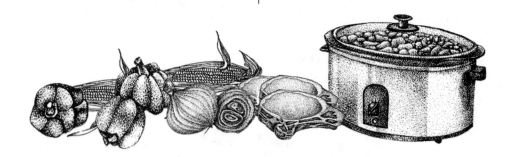

"Baked" Pork Chops

6 - 8 (½ inch thick)
    pork chops   6 - 8 (1.2 cm)
Canola oil
1 (10 ounce) can
    cream of chicken
    soup   280 g
3 tablespoons
    ketchup   50 g
1 tablespoon
    Worcestershire
    sauce   15 ml
1 onion, chopped

- Brown pork chops in a little oil in skillet and season with a little salt and pepper.

- Place pork chops in sprayed slow cooker.

- Combine chicken soup, ketchup, Worcestershire and onion in bowl and pour over pork chops.

- Cover and cook on LOW for 5 to 6 hours. Serves 6 to 8.

Delicious Pork Chops

1¾ cups flour   210 g
Scant 2 tablespoons
    dry mustard   30 ml
8 boneless, thick pork
    chops
Canola oil
1 (10 ounce) can chicken
    and rice soup   280 g

- Place flour and mustard in shallow bowl. Dredge pork chops in flour-mustard mixture.

- Brown pork chops in a little oil in skillet. Place all chops in 6-quart (6 L) oval slow cooker.

- Pour soup over pork and add about ¼ cup (60 ml) water. Cover and cook on LOW for 6 to 8 hours. Serves 6 to 8.

Country Pork Chops

7 - 8 new (red) potatoes
    with peels, sliced
2 onions, sliced
1 (10 ounce) can cream
    of celery soup   280 g
⅓ cup chicken broth   75 ml
3 tablespoons
    dijon-style mustard   45 ml
1 (4 ounce) can sliced
    mushrooms, drained   115 g
1 teaspoon minced garlic   5 ml
¾ teaspoon dried
    basil   4 ml
8 boneless pork chops
Canola oil

- Place potatoes and onions in large slow cooker.

- Combine soup, broth, mustard, mushrooms, garlic and basil in bowl, mix well and pour over potatoes and onions. Stir to coat vegetables.

- Sprinkle pork chops with a little salt and pepper. Brown pork chops in a little oil in skillet on both sides.

- Place chops over vegetables.

- Cover and cook on LOW for 6 to 7 hours. Serves 6 to 8.

Pork Roast with Apricot Glaze

1 (3 pound) boneless pork
    roast   **1.4 kg**
⅓ cup chicken broth   **75 ml**
1 (18 ounce) jar apricot
    preserves   **510 g**
2 tablespoons dijon-style
    mustard   **30 g**
1 onion, finely chopped
1 green bell pepper, seeded,
    finely chopped
Rice, cooked

- Trim fat from roast and, if necessary, cut roast to fit into sprayed 4 to 5-quart (4 to 5 L) slow cooker. Place in roast in cooker.

- Combine broth, preserves, mustard, onion and bell pepper in saucepan and heat just enough to mix ingredients well and pour over roast.

- Cover and cook on LOW for 9 to 10 hours or on HIGH for 5 to 6 hours.

- Transfer meat to serving plate.

- Sauce left in cooker is delicious as is or thicker. To thicken sauce, mix 1 tablespoon (15 ml) cornstarch and 2 tablespoons (30 ml) water. Place in saucepan and add sauce from cooker.

- Heat sauce and stir constantly until sauce thickens slightly.

- Sauce may be served with rice or just spoon over roast. Serves 6 to 8.

Show Time Pork Roast

2 onions, sliced
1 green bell pepper,
  seeded, sliced
3 pound boneless pork
  roast   1.4 kg
2 tablespoons soy sauce   30 ml
1 tablespoon ketchup   15 ml
¼ cup sugar   50 g
3 tablespoons red wine
  vinegar   45 ml
1 teaspoon minced garlic   5ml
1 (12 ounce) package egg
  noodles, cooked,
  buttered   340 g

- Arrange onion and bell pepper in sprayed slow cooker; then place roast on top.

- Combine soy sauce, ketchup, sugar, vinegar, garlic and a little salt in bowl; mix well and pour over roast.

- Cover and cook LOW heat for 6 to 8 hours or on HIGH for 3 to 4 hours. Serve over noodles. Serves 8.

Fruit-Stuffed Pork Roast

1 (3 - 3½ pound)
   boneless pork
   loin roast   1.4 - 1.6 kg
1 cup mixed dried
   fruits   160 g
1 tablespoon dried
   onion flakes   15 ml
1 teaspoon thyme
   leaves   5 ml
½ teaspoon ground
   cinnamon   2 ml
2 tablespoons canola oil 30 ml
½ cup apple cider   125 ml

- Place pork on cutting board. Cut horizontally through center of pork almost to opposite side. Open pork like a book.

- Layer dried fruits and onion flakes in opening. Bring halves of pork together and tie at 1-inch (2.5 cm) intervals with kitchen twine.

- Combine ½ teaspoon (2 ml) salt, thyme, cinnamon and ½ teaspoon (2 ml) black pepper in small bowl and rub into roast.

- Place roast in skillet with oil and brown roast on all sides.

- Place roast in sprayed slow cooker and pour apple cider in cooker.

- Cover and cook on LOW for 3 to 4 hours. Partially cool before slicing. Serves 6 to 8.

Pork with a Cranberry Glaze

1 (3 - 4 pound) pork shoulder roast	1.4 - 1.8 kg
1 (16 ounce) package frozen stew vegetables, thawed	455 g
1 (16 ounce) can whole cranberry sauce	455 g
1 (4 ounce) can chopped green chilies	115 g
¾ cup chili sauce	205 g
1 teaspoon dijon-style mustard	5 ml
2 tablespoons brown sugar	30 g

- Brown roast on all sides in sprayed skillet over medium heat. Place roast in sprayed slow cooker and top with stew vegetables.

- Combine cranberry sauce, green chilies, chili sauce, mustard and brown sugar in saucepan; heat just enough to blend ingredients. Pour mixture over roast and vegetables.

- Cover and cook on LOW heat for 8 to 9 hours or on HIGH for 4 to 4 hours 30 minutes. Transfer roast and vegetables to serving platter and keep warm.

- Strain cooking juices and skim off fat. Bring juices to a boil in medium saucepan; reduce heat and simmer for about 25 minutes or until mixture thickens. Serve sauce with sliced pork roast. Serves 6 to 8.

Tender Pork Loin

1 (3 - 4 pound) pork loin	1.4 - 1.8 kg
2 teaspoons minced garlic	10 ml
½ teaspoon rosemary	2 ml
1 teaspoon sage	5 ml
1½ teaspoons marjoram	7 ml

- Place pork loin in slow cooker, rub with minced garlic and sprinkle with rosemary, sage and marjoram. Add about ¼ cup (60 ml) water to slow cooker.

- Cover and cook on LOW heat for 4 to 5 hours. Serves 6 to 8.

TIP: *Sometimes it is hard to buy a small (3 to 4 pound/ 1.4 to 1.8 kg) pork loin, but they are available in (8 or 9 pound/3.6 to 4.1 kg) sizes. Because pork loin is such a good cut of pork (no bones - no fat), you can buy a whole loin, cut it into 2 or 3 pieces and freeze the pieces not used.*

Terrific Pork Tenderloin

2 - 3 (1 pound) pork tenderloins	2 - 3 (455 g)
1 teaspoon seasoned salt	5 ml
1 teaspoon garlic powder	5 ml
1 (4 ounce) can chopped green chilies	115 g
2 (10 ounce) cans cream of celery soup	2 (280 g)
Rice cooked	

- Place tenderloins in sprayed, oval slow cooker. Season with seasoned salt and garlic powder.

- Combine green chilies and celery soup in bowl and spoon over tenderloins, covering completely.

- Cover and cook on LOW for 8 hours. Serve over rice. Serves 2 to 3.

Spinach-Stuffed Pork Roast

1 (2 - 2½ pound) pork tenderloin	910 g
1 (10 ounce) package frozen chopped spinach, thawed	280 g
⅓ cup seasoned breadcrumbs	40 g
⅓ cup grated parmesan cheese	35 g
2 tablespoons canola oil	30 ml
½ teaspoon seasoned salt	2 ml

- Cut tenderloin horizontally lengthwise about ½-inch (1.2 cm) from top to within ¾-inch (1.8 cm) of opposite end and open flat.

- Turn pork to cut other side, from inside edge to outer edge, and open flat. If one side is thicker than other side, cover with plastic wrap and pound until both sides are ¾-inch (1.8 cm) thick.

- Squeeze spinach between paper towels to completely remove excess moisture.

- Combine spinach, breadcrumbs and cheese in bowl and mix well.

- Spread mixture on inside surfaces of pork and press down. Roll pork and tie with kitchen twine.

- Heat oil in large skillet over medium-high heat and brown pork on all sides.

- Place in oval slow cooker and sprinkle with salt. Cover and cook on LOW for 6 to 8 hours. Serves 4 to 6.

Pork and Cabbage Supper

1 (16 ounce) package baby carrots	455 g
1 cup chicken broth	250 ml
1 (1 ounce) packet golden onion soup mix	30 g
1 (3 - 4 pound) pork shoulder roast	1.4 - 1.8 kg
1 medium head cabbage	

- Place carrots in 5-quart (5 L) slow cooker.

- Add chicken broth and 1 cup (250 ml) water. Sprinkle dry soup mix and lots of black pepper over carrots.

- Cut roast in half (if needed to fit in cooker) and place over carrot mixture.

- Cover and cook on LOW for 6 to 7 hours.

- Cut cabbage in small-size chunks and place over roast. Cover and cook for an additional 1 to 2 hours or until cabbage cooks. Serves 6 to 8.

Roasted Red Pepper Tenderloin

2 pounds pork tenderloin   910 g
1 (.04 ounce) packet
    ranch dressing mix   10 g
1 cup roasted red bell
    peppers, rinsed,
    chopped   90 g
1 (8 ounce) carton sour
    cream   230 g

- Brown tenderloins in large skillet and place in 6-quart (6 L) oval slow cooker.

- Combine ranch dressing mix, red bell peppers and ½ cup (125 ml) water in bowl and spoon over tenderloins.

- Cover and cook on LOW for 4 to 5 hours.

- When ready to serve, remove tenderloins from slow cooker.

- Stir sour cream into sauce made. Serve over tenderloin slices. Serves 4 to 6.

Honey-Mustard Pork Roast

1 green bell pepper,
    seeded, chopped
1 red bell pepper, seeded,
    chopped
2 yellow onions, chopped
3 tablespoons
    refrigerated sweet
    and tangy
    honey-mustard   45 g
1 (2 - 2 ½ pound)
    pork loin roast   910 g - 1.1 kg

- Combine bell peppers and onions in 4 to 5-quart (4 to 5 L) slow cooker. Rub honey-mustard liberally over pork loin with most of honey-mustard on top; place in slow cooker.

- Cover and cook on LOW for 4 to 6 hours and place in serving platter. Spoon bell peppers, onions and pan juices in small serving bowl and spoon over slices of roast to serve. Serves 4 to 6.

Ginger Pork

1 (2 - 2½ pound) boneless pork roast	910 g
1 cup chicken broth	250 ml
3½ tablespoons quick-cooking tapioca	50 ml
3 tablespoons soy sauce	45 ml
1 teaspoon grated fresh ginger	5 ml
1 (15 ounce) can pineapple chunks with juice	425 g
1 (16 ounce) package baby carrots	455 g
1 (8 ounce) can sliced water chestnuts, drained	230 g
Rice, cooked	

- Trim fat from pork. Cut pork into 1-inch (2.5 cm) pieces, brown in large skillet and drain.

- Combine chicken broth, tapioca, soy sauce, ginger, pineapple juice, carrots and water chestnuts in sprayed 4 to 5-quart (4 to 5 L) slow cooker. (Chill pineapple chunks in refrigerator until ready to include in recipe.)

- Add browned pork. Cover and cook on LOW for 6 to 8 hours.

- Turn heat to HIGH and stir in pineapple chunks. Cover and cook for an additional 10 minutes.

- Serve over rice. Serves 4 to 6.

Barbecue Pork Roast

Use leftovers for great sandwiches.

1 onion, thinly sliced	
2 tablespoons	
flour	**15 g**
1 (2 - 3 pound) pork	
shoulder roast	**910 g - 1.4 kg**
1 (8 ounce) bottle	
barbecue sauce	**230 g**
1 tablespoon chili powder	**15 ml**
1 teaspoon ground cumin	**5 ml**

- Separate onion slices into rings and place in 4 to 5-quart 4 to 5 L) slow cooker. Sprinkle flour over onions. If necessary, cut roast to fit cooker and place over onions.

- Combine barbecue sauce, chili powder and cumin in bowl and pour over roast.

- Cover and cook on LOW for 8 to 10 hours. Remove roast from cooker and slice. Serve sauce over sliced roast. Serves 6 to 8.

TIP: To make sandwiches, shred roast and return to cooker. Cook for an additional 30 minutes to heat thoroughly.

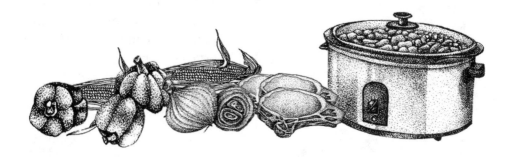

Tangy Apricot Ribs

3 - 4 pounds baby back pork ribs	1.4 - 1.8 kg
1 (16 ounce) jar apricot preserves	455 g
⅓ cup soy sauce	75 ml
¼ cup packed light brown sugar	55 g

- Place ribs in large, sprayed slow cooker.

- Combine preserves, soy sauce and brown sugar in bowl and spoon over ribs.

- Cover and cook on LOW for 6 to 8 hours. Serves 6 to 8.

Finger Lickin' Baby Backs

2½ - 3 pounds baby back pork ribs	1.1 - 1.4 kg
½ cup chili sauce	135 g
⅓ cup apple cider vinegar	75 ml
½ cup packed brown sugar	110 g

- Cut ribs in serving-size pieces, sprinkle with black pepper and place in sprayed 5 to 6-quart (5 to 6 L) slow cooker.

- Combine chili sauce, vinegar, brown sugar and about ¾ cup (175 ml) water in bowl and pour over ribs.

- Cover and cook on LOW for about 6 to 7 hours. After about 3 hours, you might move ribs around in slow cooker so sauce is spread over all ribs. Serves 4 to 6.

Delectable Apricot Ribs

4 - 5 pounds baby back pork ribs	1.8 - 2.3 kg
1 (16 ounce) jar apricot preserves	455 g
⅓ cup soy sauce	75 ml
¼ cup packed light brown sugar	55 g
2 teaspoons garlic powder	10 ml
¼ cup apple cider vinegar	60 ml

- Place ribs in sprayed slow cooker.

- Combine preserves, soy sauce, brown sugar, garlic powder and vinegar in bowl and spoon over ribs.

- Cover and cook on LOW for 6 to 7 hours. Serves 8 to 10.

Home-Style Ribs

4 - 6 pounds boneless pork spareribs	1.8 - 2.7 kg
1 cup chili sauce	270 g
1 cup packed brown sugar	220 g
2 tablespoons vinegar	30 ml
2 tablespoons Worcestershire sauce	30 ml

- Sprinkle ribs liberally with salt and pepper. Place ribs in slow cooker.

- Combine ½ cup (125 ml) water, chili sauce, brown sugar, vinegar and Worcestershire in bowl and spoon over ribs.

- Cover and cook on LOW for 5 to 6 hours. Serves 6 to 8.

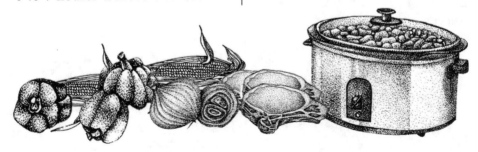

Saucy Ham Loaf

*Great with sweet and
hot mustard recipe below*

1 pound ground ham	455 g
½ pound ground beef	230 g
½ pound ground pork	230 g
2 eggs, slightly beaten	
1 cup Italian-seasoned breadcrumbs	120 g
1 (5 ounce) can evaporated milk	145 g
¼ cup chili sauce	70 g
1 teaspoon seasoned salt	5 ml

- Combine all ingredients in bowl and form into loaf in sprayed, oval slow cooker. Shape loaf so that neither end touches sides of cooker.

- Cover and cook on LOW for 6 to 7 hours. Serve with Sweet-and-Hot Mustard. Serves 4 to 6.

Sweet-and-Hot Mustard

*Use on ham loaf
or ham sandwiches.*

4 ounces dry mustard	115 g
1 cup vinegar	250 ml
3 eggs, beaten	
1 cup sugar	200 g

- Mix mustard and vinegar in bowl until smooth and let stand overnight.

- Add eggs and sugar and cook in double boiler for 8 to 10 minutes, stirring often or until it coats the spoon. Cool and store in covered jars in refrigerator. Serve with Saucy Ham Loaf.

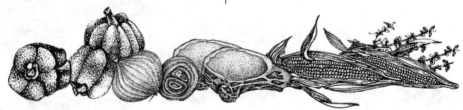

Walnut Ham

½ pound cooked ham
   slices   230 g
2 (10 ounce) cans
   cream of onion
   soup   2 (280 g)
⅓ cup grated
   parmesan cheese   35 g
⅔ cup chopped
   walnuts   90 g
Linguine, cooked

- Cut ham into ½-inch
  (1.2 cm) strips.

- Place soups, cheese, walnuts and
  ham strips in slow cooker.

- Cover and cook on LOW for
  1 to 2 hours or until hot
  and bubbly.

- Serve over linguine. Serves 4.

Sweet-and-Sour Sausage Links

2 (16 ounce) packages
   miniature smoked
   sausage links   2 (455 g)
¾ cup chili sauce   205 g
1 cup packed brown
   sugar   220 g
¼ cup horseradish   55 g

- Place sausages in 4-quart (4 L)
  slow cooker.

- Combine chili sauce, brown
  sugar and horseradish in bowl
  and pour over sausages.

- Cover and cook on LOW for
  4 hours. Serves 4 to 6.

TIP: *This can be served as an
   appetizer or served over hot,
   cooked rice.*

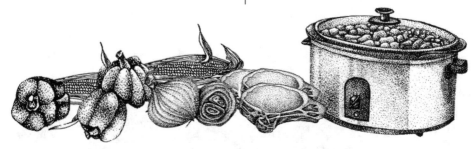

Zesty Ham Supper

1 (28 ounce) package
  frozen hash-brown
  potatoes with onions
  and peppers,
  thawed   795 g
3 cups diced cooked
  ham   420 g
1 (10 ounce) box
  frozen green peas,
  thawed   280 g
2 (10 ounce) cans
  fiesta nacho
  cheese soup   2 (280 g)
1 cup milk   250 ml
1 bunch fresh green
  onions, chopped

- Place potatoes, ham and peas in sprayed 6-quart (6 L) slow cooker and stir to mix.

- Combine soup and milk in bowl and mix well. Pour over potato mixture and mix well.

- Cover and cook on LOW for 6 to 8 hours.

- Sprinkle green onions over top when ready to serve. Serves 6 to 8.

Apricot Ham

1 (6 - 8 pound) butt or	
shank ham	2.7 - 3.6 kg
Whole cloves	
2 tablespoons dry	
mustard	30 g
1¼ cups apricot jam	400 g
1¼ cups packed light	
brown sugar	275 g

- Place ham, fat-side up in slow cooker. Stick lots of whole cloves on outside of ham.

- Combine mustard, jam and brown sugar in bowl and spread all over ham. Cover and cook on LOW for 5 to 6 hours. Serves 8 to 10.

Ben's Ham and Rice

1 (6.7 ounce) box	
brown-wild rice,	
mushroom recipe	170 g
3 - 4 cups cooked,	
chopped or cubed	
ham	420 - 560 g
1 (4 ounce) can sliced	
mushrooms,	
drained	115 g
1 (10 ounce) package	
frozen green peas	280 g
2 cups chopped celery	200 g

- Combine rice, seasoning packet, ham, mushrooms, peas, celery plus 2⅔ cups (650 ml) water in 4 to 5-quart (4 to 5 L) slow cooker. Stir to mix well.

- Cover and cook on LOW for 2 to 4 hours. Serves 4 to 6.

Ham Loaf

Great for leftover ham

1½ pounds cooked, ground ham	680 g
1 pound ground turkey	455 g
2 eggs	
1 cup seasoned breadcrumbs	120 g
2 teaspoons chicken seasoning	10 ml

- In bowl, combine ground ham, ground turkey, eggs, seasoned breadcrumb and chicken seasoning in bowl and mix well.

- Use hands to pick up loaf mixture and shape into short loaf that will fit into oval slow cooker.

- Cover and cook on LOW for 4 to 5 hours.

- Serve with Cherry Sauce. Serves 4 to 6.

Cherry Sauce:

1 cup cherry preserves	320 g
2 tablespoons cider vinegar	30 ml
Scant ⅛ teaspoon ground cloves	.5 ml
Scant ⅛ teaspoon ground cinnamon	.5 ml

- Place cherry preserves, vinegar, cloves and cinnamon in saucepan and heat. Serve over slices of Ham Loaf.

Special Ham Supper

2½ cups cooked, ground ham	350 g
⅔ cup finely crushed cheese crackers	40 g
1 large egg	
⅓ cup hot and spicy ketchup	90 g
¼ cup (½ stick) butter	60 g
1 (18 ounce) package frozen hash-brown potatoes, thawed	510 g
1 onion, coarsely chopped	
1 (5 ounce) can evaporated milk	145 g
1½ cups shredded Monterey Jack cheese	175 g
½ teaspoon paprika	2 ml

- Combine ground ham, crackers, egg and ketchup in bowl and shape into 6 patties.

- Melt butter in skillet and cook potatoes and onion on medium heat for about 10 minutes, turning frequently to prevent browning. Drain and transfer to sprayed slow cooker.

- Combine milk, cheese, paprika and a little salt and pepper in bowl.

- Pour mixture over potatoes and onions. Place ham patties on top; cover and cook on LOW for 3 to 5 hours. Serves 6.

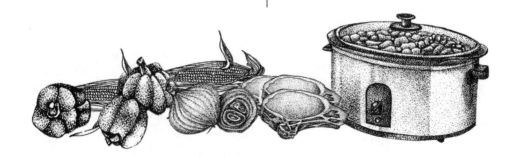

Ham and Potato Dish

4 large baking potatoes, peeled

3 cups cubed leftover ham   420 g

1 (10 ounce) box frozen whole kernel corn, drained   280 g

1 (10 ounce) package frozen onion-pepper blend, thawed   280 g

1 teaspoon seasoned salt   5 ml

2 (10 ounce) cans fiesta nacho cheese soup   2 (280 g)

½ cup milk   125 ml

1 (3 ounce) can fried onion rings   85 g

- Cut potatoes into 1-inch (2.5 cm) cubes.

- Combine potatoes, ham, corn, onions and peppers and seasoned salt in slow cooker.

- Heat cheese soup and milk in saucepan just enough to mix well. Add to slow cooker and mix with ingredients.

- Cover and cook on LOW for 5 to 6 hours or until potatoes are tender. When ready to serve, sprinkle onions over top. Serves 4 to 6.

Creamy Potatoes and Ham

5 medium potatoes, peeled, sliced, divided	
1 onion, chopped, divided	
2 cups cooked, cubed ham, divided	280 g
1 (8 ounce) package cubed Velveeta® cheese, divided	230 g
1 (10 ounce) can broccoli-cheese soup	280 g
¼ cup milk	60 ml

- Layer half each of potatoes, 1 teaspoon (5 ml) salt, onion, ham and cheese in slow cooker and repeat layer.

- Combine soup and milk in bowl until fairly smooth and add to slow cooker.

- Cover and cook on HIGH for 1 hour. Reduce heat to LOW and cook for 6 to 7 hours. Serves 4.

Creamed Ham with Spaghetti

2 (10 ounce) cans cream of mushroom soup with roasted garlic	2 (280 g)
1 cup sliced fresh mushrooms	70 g
2 - 2½ cups cooked, cubed ham	280 - 350 g
1 (5 ounce) can evaporated milk	145 g
1 (7 ounce) box ready-cut spaghetti	200 g

- Combine soups, mushrooms, ham, evaporated milk and a little salt and pepper in slow cooker.

- Cover and cook on LOW for 2 hours and mix well.

- Cook spaghetti in saucepan and drain. Add spaghetti to slow cooker and toss to coat. Serves 4 to 6.

Ham to the Rescue

2½ cups cooked, ground ham	350 g
⅔ cup crushed white cheddar Cheez-Its® crackers	40 g
1 large egg	
⅓ cup chili sauce	90 g
4 medium potatoes, peeled, sliced	
Canola oil	
1 green bell pepper, cored, seeded, julienned	
1 (8 ounce) package shredded cheddar-Jack cheese	230 g
1 (5 ounce) can evaporated milk	145 g
1 teaspoon seasoned salt	5 ml

- Combine ham, crushed crackers, egg and chili sauce in bowl and mix well.

- Shape ham mixture into 6 patties and set aside.

- Saute potatoes in a little oil in skillet and turn several times to brown lightly on both sides. Place potatoes and bell pepper in 6-quart (6 L) slow cooker.

- In separate bowl, combine cheese, evaporated milk and seasoned salt and pour over potatoes.

- Place ham patties over potatoes.

- Cover and cook on LOW for 3 to 4 hours. Serves 4 to 6.

Ham and Potato Casserole

3 - 4 large potatoes, peeled,
  thinly sliced
1 (8 ounce) package
  shredded cheddar
  cheese   230 g
½ cup chopped onion   80 g
½ cup chopped green bell
  pepper   75 g
2 ribs celery, sliced
2 cups cooked, chopped
  ham   280 g
1 (10 ounce) can cream
  of chicken soup   280 g
⅔ cup milk   150 ml
1 teaspoon seasoned salt   5 ml

- Place potatoes, cheese, onion, bell pepper, celery and ham in sprayed slow cooker and mix well.

- Combine soup, milk and seasoned salt in small bowl and pour evenly over potato-vegetable mixture.

- Cover and cook on HIGH for 4 hours. Serves 8.

Tortellini Italian-Style

2 pounds bulk Italian
    sausage   910 g
1 (15 ounce) carton
    refrigerated marinara
    sauce   425 g
2 cups sliced fresh
    mushrooms, sliced   145 g
1 (15 ounce) cans Italian
    stewed tomatoes   425 g
1 (9 ounce) package
    refrigerated cheese
    tortellini   255 g
1½ cups shredded
    mozzarella cheese   170 g

- Brown and cook sausage in skillet for 10 to 15 minutes and drain well.

- Combine sausage, marinara sauce, mushrooms and tomatoes in sprayed 5-quart (5 L) slow cooker.

- Cover and cook on LOW 6 to 7 hours. Stir in tortellini.

- Cover and cook on HIGH for about 15 minutes or until tortellini is tender. When ready to serve, sprinkle with cheese. Serves 4 to 6.

Celebrated Sausage and Rice

1 (16 ounce) Polish sausage ring, cut into ¼-inch slices	455 g/6 mm
2 (15 ounce) cans Italian stewed tomatoes	2 (425 g)
1 (16 ounce) package frozen chopped onions and bell peppers	455 g
2 ribs celery, sliced	
1 teaspoon Italian seasoning	5 ml
1 teaspoon dried basil	5 ml
½ teaspoon hot pepper sauce	2 ml
1½ cups instant rice	145 g

- Layer sausage, stewed tomatoes, onions and bell peppers, and celery in sprayed slow cooker.

- Sprinkle with Italian seasoning, basil and pepper sauce. Cover and cook on LOW for 7 hours.

- Stir in rice and ½ cup (125 ml) water and cook for an additional 30 minutes. Serves 4 to 5.

Sausage and Beans

1 (1 pound) fully cooked smoked, link sausage	455 g
2 (15 ounce) cans baked beans	2 (425 g)
1 (15 ounce) can great northern beans, drained	425 g
1 (15 ounce) can pinto beans, drained	425 g
½ cup chili sauce	135 g
⅔ cup packed brown sugar	150 g
1 tablespoon Worcestershire sauce	15 ml

- Cut link sausage into 1-inch (2.5 cm) slices. Layer sausage and beans in slow cooker.

- Combine chili sauce, brown sugar, a little black pepper and Worcestershire sauce in bowl and pour over beans and sausage.

- Cover and cook on LOW for 4 hours. Stir before serving. Serves 4.

Sauerkraut and Bratwurst

1 (28 ounce) jar
    refrigerated
    sauerkraut   795 g
¾ cup beer   175 ml
1 tablespoon marinade
    for chicken
    (Lea & Perrins)   15 ml
1 (1 ounce) packet onion
    soup mix   30 g
2 pounds pre-cooked
    bratwurst   910 g

- Combine sauerkraut, beer, Worcestershire and onion soup mix in 4 to 5-quart (4 to 5 L) slow cooker and mix well.

- Cut bratwurst in diagonal slices and place on top of sauerkraut-beer mixture.

- Cover and cook on LOW for 5 to 6 hours or on HIGH for 2 hours 30 minutes to 3 hours. Serves 4 to 6.

Tuna OK Bake

2 (6 ounce) cans white
    tuna, drained,
    flaked   2 (170 g)
1 (10 ounce) can cream
    of chicken soup   280 g
3 eggs, hard-boiled,
    chopped
3 ribs celery, thinly
    sliced
1 red bell pepper,
    seeded, chopped
½ cup coarsely
    chopped pecans   55 g
½ cup mayonnaise   110 g
1 teaspoon white
    pepper   5 ml
2 cups crushed potato
    chips, divided   110 g

- Combine tuna, soup, eggs, celery, bell pepper, pecans, mayonnaise, white pepper, 1 cup (60 g) potato chips and a little salt in bowl and mix well. Transfer to sprayed slow cooker.

- Cover and cook on LOW for 5 to 7 hours. When ready to serve, sprinkle remaining potato chips on top. Serves 4 to 5.

Cheddar Crab Casserole

3 tablespoons butter	45 g
2 ribs celery, thinly sliced	
1 (10 ounce) package frozen chopped onions and bell peppers	280 g
4 tablespoons flour	30 g
2 (14 ounce) cans chicken broth	2 (400 g)
1¼ cups instant rice	145 g
2 (6 ounce) cans crabmeat, drained, flaked	2 (170 g)
1 cup shredded cheddar cheese	115 g
1 (4 ounce) can sliced mushrooms, drained	115 g
½ cup sliced almonds	95 g
1 cup seasoned breadcrumbs	120 g
¼ cup (½ stick) butter, melted	60 g

- Melt butter in skillet on medium heat and lightly saute celery and onions and bell peppers. Add flour and stir well. Slowly add chicken broth, stirring constantly and cook until slightly thickened.

- Combine rice, crabmeat, cheese, mushrooms and almonds in bowl. Stir in sauce and transfer to sprayed slow cooker. Cover and cook on HIGH for 3 to 5 hours.

- Spoon contents of slow cooker into shallow glass serving dish.

- Combine breadcrumbs and melted butter in small bowl; sprinkle over contents in serving dish. Place under broiler until crumbs are slightly brown. Serves 5 to 6.

Desserts

Breaded, Fondued, Fruited & Fudged

Desserts Contents

Delicious Bread Pudding. 295
Bread Pudding with Coconut
     and Nuts. 296
Pineapple-Rice Pudding 296
Baked Apples 297
Butter-Baked Apples. 298
Peachy-Cranberry Delight. 298
Fresh Peach Cobbler 299

Peaches with Crunch. 299
Cran-Apples for Pound Cake. 300
Surprise Dessert 300
Chocolate Fondue 301
Magnificent Fudge 302
Chocolate Delight. 303
Fruit Sauce .303

Delicious Bread Pudding

8 cups cubed leftover hot rolls, cinnamon rolls or bread	280 g
2 cups milk	500 ml
4 large eggs	
¾ cup sugar	150 g
⅓ cup packed brown sugar	75 g
¼ cup (½ stick) butter, melted	60 g
1 teaspoon vanilla	5 ml
¼ teaspoon ground nutmeg	1 ml
1 cup finely chopped pecans	110 g
Lemons sauce or whipped topping	

- Place cubed bread or rolls in sprayed slow cooker.

- Combine, milk eggs, sugar, brown sugar, butter, vanilla and nutmeg in bowl and beat until smooth. Stir in pecans. Add to slow cooker.

- Cover and cook on LOW for 3 hours. Serve with lemon sauce or whipped topping. Serves 6.

Bread Pudding with Coconut and Nuts

1 cup sugar	200 g
½ cup (1 stick) butter, softened	115 g
1 teaspoon ground cinnamon	5 ml
4 eggs	
3 cups white bread cubes	105 g
⅓ cup flaked coconut	30 g
⅓ cup chopped pecans	40 g

- Beat sugar, butter and cinnamon in bowl. Add eggs and beat well until it blends. Stir in bread, coconut and pecans. Pour into 4 to 5-quart (4 to 5 L) slow cooker.

- Cover and cook on LOW for 3 to 4 hours or on HIGH 1 hour 30 minutes to 2 hours or until knife inserted in center comes out clean. Serves 8.

TIP: *Serve pudding warm with caramel ice cream topping, if desired.*

Pineapple-Rice Pudding

1 cup cooked white rice	185 g
¾ cup sugar	150 g
1 (1 pint) carton half-and-half cream	500 ml
1 tablespoon cornstarch	15 ml
3 eggs, beaten	
1 teaspoon vanilla	5 ml
1 (15 ounce) can crushed pineapple with juice	425 g
Pecan, chopped, toasted	

- Combine rice, sugar and half-and-half cream in bowl and mix well.

- Stir in cornstarch, eggs, vanilla and pineapple.

- Pour into sprayed 4 to 5-quart (4 to 5 L) slow cooker.

- Cover and cook on LOW for 2 to 3 hours.

- When ready to serve, top each serving with toasted, chopped pecans as a special touch. Serves 6.

Baked Apples

4 - 5 large baking apples
1 tablespoon lemon juice   **15 ml**
⅓ cup Craisins®   **40 g**
½ cup chopped pecans   **55 g**
¾ cup packed brown
**   sugar**   **165 g**
½ teaspoon ground
**   cinnamon**   **2 ml**
¼ cup (½ stick) butter,
**   melted**   **60 g**
Caramel ice cream
**   topping**

- Scoop out center of each apple and leave cavity about ½ inch (1.2 cm) from bottom.

- Peel top of apples down about 1 inch (2.5 cm) and brush lemon juice on peeled edges.

- Combine Craisins®, pecans, brown sugar, cinnamon and butter in bowl. Spoon mixture into apple cavities.

- Pour ½ cup (125 ml) water in oval slow cooker and place apples on bottom.

- Cover and cook on LOW for 1 to 3 hours or until tender.

- Serve warm or room temperature drizzled with caramel ice cream topping. Serves 5.

Butter Baked Apples

6 large green baking
    apples
2 tablespoons lemon
    juice   30 ml
¼ cup (½ stick) butter,
    melted   60 g
1 cup packed brown
    sugar   220 g
1 teaspoon ground
    cinnamon   5 ml
½ teaspoon ground
    nutmeg   2 ml
Vanilla ice cream

- Peel, core, cut apples in half horizontally and place in slow cooker.

- Drizzle with lemon juice and butter. Sprinkle with brown sugar, cinnamon and nutmeg.

- Cover and cook on LOW for 2 hours 30 minutes to 3 hours 30 minutes or on HIGH for 1 hour 30 minutes to 2 hours.

- Serve with vanilla ice cream. Serves 6.

Peachy-Cranberry Delight

1½ cups quick-cooking
    oats   120 g
1 (16 ounce) box brown
    sugar   455 g
⅔ cup sugar   135 g
¾ cup biscuit mix   90 g
2 teaspoons ground
    cinnamon   10 ml
½ cup orange juice 125 ml
1 (16 ounce) package
    frozen sliced peaches,
    thawed   455 g
1 (6 ounce) package
    Craisins®   170 g

- Combine oats, brown sugar, sugar, biscuit mix, cinnamon and orange juice in large bowl. Gently stir in peaches and cranberries. Spoon into sprayed slow cooker.

- Cover and cook on LOW for 5 hours. Serve while still warm. Serves 10.

Fresh Peach Cobbler

1 cup sugar	200 g
¾ cup biscuit mix	90 g
2 eggs	
2 teaspoons vanilla	10 ml
1 (5 ounce) can	
evaporated milk	145 g
2 tablespoons butter,	
melted	30 g
3 large, ripe peaches,	
peeled, mashed	
Peach ice cream	

- Combine sugar and biscuit mix in large bowl, stir in eggs, vanilla, evaporated milk and butter and mix well.

- Fold in peaches, pour into sprayed slow cooker and stir well.

- Cover and cook on LOW for 6 to 8 hours or on HIGH for 3 to 4 hours.

- Serve warm with peach ice cream. Serves 6.

Peaches with Crunch

¾ cup old-fashioned	
oats	60 g
⅔ cup packed brown	
sugar	150 g
¾ cup sugar	150 g
½ cup biscuit mix	60 g
½ teaspoon ground	
cinnamon	2 ml
2 (15 ounce) cans	
sliced peaches,	
well drained	2 (425 g)

- Combine oats, brown sugar, sugar, biscuit mix and cinnamon in bowl.

- Stir in drained peaches and spoon into sprayed 3 to 4-quart (3 to 4 L) slow cooker.

- Cover and cook on LOW for 4 to 5 hours. Serve in sherbet dishes. Serves 6.

Cran-Apples for Pound Cake

1 (6 ounce) package dried
    apples   170 g
½ cup Craisins®
3 cups cranberry juice
    cocktail   710 ml
¾ cup packed brown
    sugar   180 ml
2 cinnamon sticks, halved
Pound cake or vanilla ice
    cream

- Add apples, Craisins®, juice, brown sugar and cinnamon sticks to sprayed 3 to 4-quart (3 to 4 L) slow cooker.

- Cover and cook on LOW for 4 to 5 hours or until liquid absorbs and fruit is tender.

- Serve warm, at room temperature or chilled over slices of pound cake or vanilla ice cream. Serves 6.

Surprise Dessert

1 (18 ounce) box spice
    cake mix   510 g
1 cup butterscotch chips 170 g
4 eggs, slightly beaten
¾ cup canola oil   175 ml
1 (3.4 ounce) package
    butterscotch instant
    pudding mix   100 g
1 (8 ounce) carton sour
    cream   230 g
1 cup chopped pecans   110 g
Butter-pecan ice cream

- Combine all ingredients and ¾ cup (175 ml) water in large bowl. Pour into sprayed 4 to 5-quart (4 to 5 L) slow cooker.

- Cover and cook on LOW for 6 to 7 hours or on HIGH for 3 hours to 3 hours 30 minutes. Serve hot or room temperature with butter-pecan ice cream. Serves 8.

Chocolate Fondue

*Use the slow cooker
as a fondue pot.*

2 (7 ounce) chocolate
    bars, chopped   **2 (200 g)**
2 (2 ounce) bars
    white chocolate,
    chopped   **2 (60 g)**
1 (7 ounce) jar
    marshmallow
    creme   **200 g**
¾ cup half-and-half
    cream   **175 ml**
½ cup slivered
    almonds,
    chopped, toasted   **40 g**
¼ cup amaretto   **60 ml**
Pound cake

- Combine broken chocolate bars, white chocolate bar, marshmallow creme, half-and-half cream and almonds in small, sprayed slow cooker.

- Cover and cook on LOW for about 2 hours or until chocolates melt. Stir to mix well and fold in amaretto. Serves 6 to 8.

TIP: Use slow cooker as fondue pot or transfer chocolate mixture to fondue pot. Cut pound cake into small squares and use to dip into fondue.

Magnificent Fudge

2 (16 ounce) jars
   slightly salted,
   dry-roasted
   peanuts   2 (455 g)
1 (12 ounce) package
   semi-sweet
   chocolate chips   340 g
1 (4 ounce) bar
   German
   chocolate, broken 115 g
2 (24 ounce)
   packages white
   chocolate bark
   or (3 pounds)
   almond bark,
   chopped   2 (680 g)/1.4 kg

- Place peanuts in sprayed 5-quart (5 L) slow cooker. In layers, add chocolate chips, German chocolate and white chocolate bark.

- Cover and cook on LOW for 3 hours without removing lid. When candy cooks 3 hours, remove lid, stir and cool in covered slow cooker. Stir again and drop teaspoonfuls onto wax paper. Serves 8 to 10.

TIP: *For darker fudge, use 1 white bark and 1 dark bark.*

Chocolate Delight

1 (18 ounce) box chocolate cake mix	510 g
1 (8 ounce) carton sour cream	230 g
4 eggs	
¾ cup canola oil	175 ml
1 (3.4 ounce) box instant chocolate pudding mix	100 g
¾ cup chopped pecans	85 g
Vanilla ice cream	

- Mix cake mix, sour cream, eggs, oil, pudding mix, pecans and 1 cup (250 ml) water in bowl. Pour into sprayed slow cooker.

- Cover and cook on LOW for 6 to 8 hours. Serve hot or warm with vanilla ice cream. Serves 8.

Fruit Sauce

8 cups fresh fruit, thinly sliced	1.3 kg
⅓ cup packed brown sugar	75 g
⅓ cup sugar	70 g
2 tablespoons quick-cooking tapioca	30 ml
1 teaspoon grated fresh ginger	5 ml
⅔ cup Craisins® or cherries	80 g
Pound cake or ice cream	

- Combine fruit, juice, brown sugar, sugar, tapioca and ginger in 4-quart (4 L) slow cooker. Cover and cook on LOW for 4 hours. Add Craisins® or cherries and mix well.

- Cover and let stand for 10 to 15 minutes. To serve, spoon over slices of pound cake or ice cream. Serves 8.

Index

A

A Different Bean   106
A Different Corned Beef   159
A Different Stew   69
Abundant Stuffed Shells   174
Appetizers
   Broccoli Dip   10
   Bubbly Franks   24
   Cheesy Bacon Dip   11
   Chicken-Enchilada Dip   14
   Crab-Artichoke Spread   20
   Crab Dip   9
   Firecrackers and Bacon   18
   Great Balls of Fire   19
   Hamburger Dip   12
   Hot Broccoli Dip   13
   Hot Reuben Spread   19
   Hot Southwest Dip   10
   Indian-Corn Dip   13
   Party Smokies   20
   Pepperoni Dip   15
   Sausage-Hamburger Dip   16
   Sausage-Pineapple Bits   21
   Spicy Franks   24
   Teriyaki Wingettes   22
   The Big Dipper   17
   Unbelievable Crab Dip   9
   Whiz Bang Dip   17
   Wingettes in Honey Sauce   23
Apricot Chicken   183
Apricot Ham   281
Arroz con Pollo   239
Artichoke-Chicken Pasta   184
Asparagus-Cheese Chicken   236

B

Bacon-Wrapped Chicken   185
Baked Apples   297
"Baked" Chicken   223
"Baked" Pork Chops   264
Barbecue Pork Roast   275
Beans and Barley Soup   64
Beans and More Beans   106
Beans 'n Sausage Soup   65
Beef
   A Different Corned Beef   159
   Abundant Stuffed Shells   174
   Beef and Gravy   177
   Beef and Macaroni Supper   172
   Beef and Noodles al Grande   161
   Beef-Bean Medley   173
   Beef Ribs and Gravy   155
   Beef Roast   152
   Beef Roulades   143

Beef Tips and Mushrooms Supreme 149
Beef Tips over Noodles 144
Beef Tips over Pasta 145
Beefy Onion Supper 142
Brisket and Gravy 156
Cheeseburger Supper 171
Classic Beef Roast 151
Cola Roast 141
Cowboy Feed 170
Fiesta Beef and Rice 169
Good Brisket 154
Hash Brown Dinner 168
Herb-Crusted Beef Roast 150
Italian Steak 141
Italian Tortellini 176
Italy's Best 175
Jack's Meat Loaf 167
Justice with Short Ribs 160
Mac 'n Cheese Supper 165
Make-Believe Lasagna 164
Meat and Potatoes 155
Meat on the Table 166
Mushroom Beef 151
Mushroom-Round Steak 140
O'Brian's Hash 140
Old-Time Pot Roast 148
Pepper Steak 136
Pot Roast and Veggies 146
Sauce for Fancy Meatballs 162
Savory Steak 135

Shredded Brisket for Sandwiches 157
Sloppy Joes 177
Smoked Brisket 153
Southwest Spaghetti 162
Special Hot Dog Supper 178
Spicy Swiss Steak 137
Stroganoff 138
Stuffed Cabbage 163
Sweet and Savory Brisket 154
Sweet-and-Sour Beef 147
Swiss Steak 135
Teriyaki Steak 139
The Best Ever Brisket 158
Beef and Barley Soup 64
Beef and Black Bean Soup 62
Beef and Gravy 177
Beef and Macaroni Supper 172
Beef and Noodle Soup 63
Beef and Noodles al Grande 161
Beef-Bean Medley 173
Beef Ribs and Gravy 155
Beef Roast 152
Beef Roulades 143
Beef Tips and Mushrooms Supreme 149
Beef Tips over Noodles 144
Beef Tips over Pasta 145
Beefy Onion Supper 142
Beefy Rice Soup 61
Ben's Ham and Rice 281
Better Butter Beans 107

Black Bean Soup   53
Black-Eyed Soup   61
Bread Pudding with Coconut and Nuts   296
Brisket and Gravy   156
Broccoli and Cheese   100
Broccoli-Cheese Bake   99
Broccoli-Cheese Chicken   186
Broccoli Dip   10
Broccoli-Rice Chicken   183
Bubbly Franks   24
Butter Baked Apples   298

C

Cajun Bean Soup   60
Cajun Beans and Rice   105
California Vegetables   119
Carnival Couscous   131
Celebrated Sausage and Rice   289
Cheddar Crab Casserole   292
Cheddar Soup Plus   60
Cheese-Please Spinach   116
Cheese-Spaghetti and Spinach   132
Cheeseburger Supper   171
Cheesy Bacon Dip   11
Cheesy Chicken and Noodles   237
Cheesy Potato Soup   58
Cheesy Ranch Potatoes   128
Cheezy Potatoes   126
Chicken Alfredo   232

Chicken and Barley Soup   56
Chicken and Everything Good   231
Chicken and Noodles   187
Chicken and Pasta   188
Chicken and Rice Soup   56
Chicken and Stuffing   230
Chicken & Turkey
  Apricot Chicken   183
  Arroz con Pollo   239
  Artichoke-Chicken Pasta   184
  Asparagus-Cheese Chicken   236
  Bacon-Wrapped Chicken   185
  "Baked" Chicken   223
  Broccoli-Cheese Chicken   186
  Broccoli-Rice Chicken   183
  Cheesy Chicken and Noodles   237
  Chicken Alfredo   232
  Chicken and Everything Good   231
  Chicken and Noodles   187
  Chicken and Pasta   188
  Chicken and Stuffing   230
  Chicken and Vegetables   189
  Chicken Breast Deluxe   196
  Chicken Cacciatore   227
  Chicken Coq au Vin   226
  Chicken Curry over Rice   185
  Chicken Delicious   190
  Chicken Delight   191
  Chicken Dinner   192
  Chicken Fajitas   193

Chicken for Supper   194
Chicken for the Gods   182
Chicken Marseilles   195
Chicken Olé   182
Chicken-Ready Supper   194
Chicken Supper   197
Chicken-Supper Ready   192
Chicken with Orange Sauce   222
Chow Mein Chicken   198
Classy Chicken Dinner   199
Colorful Rice and Turkey   245
Cream Cheese Chicken   186
Creamed Chicken   200
Creamed Chicken and Vegetables   201
Creamy Chicken and Potatoes   199
Creamy Salsa Chicken   202
Delicious Chicken Pasta   204
Delightful Chicken and Veggies   202
Farmhouse Supper   205
Golden Chicken Dinner   206
Hawaiian Chicken   207
Here's the Stuff   208
Honey-Baked Chicken   221
Imperial Chicken   207
Italian Chicken   235
Lemon Chicken   225
Maple-Plum Glazed Turkey Breast   233
Monterey Bake   229
Mushroom Chicken   209
Orange Chicken   210

Oregano Chicken   210
Perfect Chicken Breasts   212
Picante Chicken   211
Quick-Fix Chicken   211
Russian Chicken   213
Saffron Rice and Chicken   224
Sausage and Rice   246
Savory Chicken Fettuccini   215
Scrumptious Chicken Breasts   216
Slow Cooker Cordon Bleu   203
Smothered Chicken Breasts   217
So-Good Chicken   213
Southern Chicken   234
Southwestern Chicken Pot   218
Stupendous Rice and Chicken   238
Sunday Chicken   219
Sweet-and-Sour Chicken   218
Sweet and Spicy Chicken   233
Taco Chicken   228
Tangy Chicken   221
Tangy Chicken Legs   228
Tasty Chicken and Veggies   223
Tasty Chicken-Rice and Veggies   220
Three Hour Chicken   239
Turkey Bake   241
Turkey Cassoulet   244
Turkey Loaf   242
Turkey Spaghetti   243
Winter Dinner   214
Yes to This Chicken   240

Chicken and Vegetables   189

Chicken Breast Deluxe   196

Chicken Cacciatore   227

Chicken Chowder   91

Chicken Coq au Vin   226

Chicken Curry over Rice   185

Chicken Delicious   190

Chicken Delight   191

Chicken Dinner   192

Chicken-Enchilada Dip   14

Chicken Fajitas   193

Chicken for Supper   194

Chicken for the Gods   182

Chicken Marseilles   195

Chicken Olé   182

Chicken-Pasta Soup   57

Chicken-Ready Supper   194

Chicken Stew   69

Chicken Stew over Biscuits   80

Chicken Supper   197

Chicken-Supper Ready   192

Chicken-Tortellini Stew   66

Chicken with Orange Sauce   222

Chili Frijoles   109

Chili Soup   55

Chocolate Delight   303

Chocolate Fondue   301

Chow Mein Chicken   198

Chunky Chili   87

Cinnamon Carrots   110

Classic Beef Roast   151

Classy Chicken Dinner   199

Cola Roast   141

Colorful Rice and Turkey   245

Comfort Stew   79

Company Broccoli   101

Company Potatoes   126

Confetti-Chicken Soup   54

Corn-Ham Chowder   93

Country Chicken Chowder   90

Country Pork Chops   265

Cowboy Feed   170

Crab-Artichoke Spread   20

Crab Chowder   89

Crab Dip   9

Cran-Apples for Pound Cake   300

Cream Cheese Chicken   186

Cream of Zucchini Soup   52

Creamed Cheese Spinach   115

Creamed Chicken   200

Creamed Chicken and Vegetables   201

Creamed Ham with Spaghetti   285

Creamed New Potatoes   120

Creamed Peas and Potatoes   115

Creamy Chicken and Potatoes   199

Creamy Limas   108

Creamy Potatoes and Ham   285

Creamy Salsa Chicken   202

Creamy Vegetable Soup   51
Crunchy Couscous   130
Crunchy Green Beans   105

D

Delectable Apricot Ribs   277
Delicious Bread Pudding   295
Delicious Broccoli-Cheese Soup   43
Delicious Chicken Pasta   204
Delicious Pork Chops   264
Delicious Risotto Rice   130
Delightful Chicken and Veggies   202
Desserts
 Baked Apples   297
 *Bread Pudding with Coconut and
   Nuts   296*
 Butter Baked Apples   298
 Chocolate Delight   303
 Chocolate Fondue   301
 Cran-Apples for Pound Cake   300
 Delicious Bread Pudding   295
 Fresh Peach Cobbler   299
 Fruit Sauce   303
 Magnificent Fudge   302
 Peaches with Crunch   299
 Peachy-Cranberry Delight   298
 Pineapple-Rice Pudding   296
 Surprise Dessert   300
Dressed-Up Hash Browns   125

E

Easy Baked Potatoes   124
Easy Chili   86
Enchilada Soup   48

F

Farmhouse Supper   205
Fiesta Beef and Rice   169
Finger Lickin' Baby Backs   276
Firecrackers and Bacon   18
Four Veggie Bake   118
French Onion Soup   46
Fresh Peach Cobbler   299
Fruit Sauce   303
Fruit-Stuffed Pork Roast   268

G

Ginger Pork   274
Glazed Sweet Potatoes   128
Glory Potatoes   124
Golden Chicken Dinner   206
Golden Squash   113
Golden Veggies   118
Good Brisket   154
Good Old Cheesy Potatoes   123
Good Time Chops, Tators and Peas   250
Great Balls of Fire   19

Green Bean Revenge   104
Green Beans to Enjoy   103

H

Ham and Cabbage Stew   77
Ham and Potato Casserole   287
Ham and Potato Dish   284
Ham, Bean and Pasta Soup   45
Ham Loaf   282
Ham to the Rescue   286
Ham-Vegetable Chowder   88
Hamburger Dip   12
Hamburger Soup   49
Harvest-Vegetable Casserole   117
Hash Brown Dinner   168
Hawaiian Chicken   207
Healthy Veggies   117
Hearty Meatball Stew   77
Herb-Crusted Beef Roast   150
Here's the Stuff   208
Home-Style Ribs   277
Honey-Baked Chicken   221
Honey-Mustard Pork Chops   263
Honey-Mustard Pork Roast   273
Hoppin' John   129
Hot Broccoli Dip   13
Hot Reuben Spread   19
Hot Southwest Dip   10
Hungarian Stew   76

I

Imperial Chicken   207
Indian-Corn Dip   13
Italian Bean Soup   44
Italian Beans   107
Italian Chicken   235
Italian Pork Chops   262
Italian Steak   141
Italian Tortellini   176
Italian-Vegetable Stew   76
Italy's Best   175

J

Jack's Meat Loaf   167
Justice with Short Ribs   160

K

Krazy Karrots   111

L

Lemon Chicken   225

M

Mac 'n Cheese Supper   165
Magnificent Fudge   302
Make-Believe Lasagna   164

Maple-Plum Glazed Turkey Breast   233

Meat and Potatoes   155

Meat on the Table   166

Meatball and Veggie Stew   75

Meatball Soup   42

Meatball Stew   75

Mexican-Meatball Soup   28

Minestrone Soup   66

Monterey Bake   229

Mushroom Beef   151

Mushroom Chicken   209

Mushroom-Round Steak   140

N

Navy Bean Soup   41

O

O'Brian's Hash   140

Old-Time Pot Roast   148

Olé! For Stew   74

Orange Chicken   210

Oregano Chicken   210

Oyster Chowder   92

P

Pancho Villa Stew   68

Party Smokies   20

Pasta-Veggie Soup   40

Peaches with Crunch   299

Peachy Pork Chops   261

Peachy-Cranberry Delight   298

Pepper Steak   136

Pepperoni Dip   15

Perfect Chicken Breasts   212

Picante Chicken   211

Pineapple-Pork Chops   260

Pineapple-Rice Pudding   296

Pinto Bean-Vegetable Soup   43

Pizza Soup   39

Pork

Apricot Ham   281

"Baked" Pork Chops   264

Barbecue Pork Roast   275

Ben's Ham and Rice   281

Celebrated Sausage and Rice   289

Country Pork Chops   265

Creamed Ham with Spaghetti   285

Creamy Potatoes and Ham   285

Delectable Apricot Ribs   277

Delicious Pork Chops   264

Finger Lickin' Baby Backs   276

Fruit-Stuffed Pork Roast   268

Ginger Pork   274

Good Time Chops, Tators and Peas   250

Ham and Potato Casserole   287

Ham and Potato Dish   284

Ham Loaf   282

Ham to the Rescue   286

Home-Style Ribs   277
Honey-Mustard Pork Chops   263
Honey-Mustard Pork Roast   273
Italian Pork Chops   262
Peachy Pork Chops   261
Pineapple-Pork Chops   260
Pork and Cabbage Supper   272
Pork Chops and Gravy   257
Pork Chops Deluxe   252
Pork Chops for Supper   256
Pork Chops Pizza   258
Pork Chops with Orange Sauce   254
Pork Roast with Apricot Glaze   266
Pork with a Cranberry Glaze   269
Promising Pork Chops   259
Ranch Pork Chops   253
Roasted Red Pepper Tenderloin   273
Saucy Ham Loaf   278
Sauerkraut and Bratwurst   291
Sausage and Beans   290
Savory Pork Chops   253
Show Time Pork Roast   267
Smothered Pork Chop Dinner   251
Special Ham Supper   283
Spinach-Stuffed Pork Roast   271
Stuffed Pork Chops   249
Sweet-and-Hot Mustard   278
Sweet-and-Sour Sausage Links   279
Tangy Apricot Ribs   276
Tender Pork Loin   270

Terrific Pork Tenderloin   270
Tortellini Italian-Style   288
Walnut Ham   279
Western Pork Supper   255
Zesty Ham Supper   280
Pork and Cabbage Supper   272
Pork and Hominy Soup   38
Pork Chops and Gravy   257
Pork Chops Deluxe   252
Pork Chops for Supper   256
Pork Chops Pizza   258
Pork Chops with Orange Sauce   254
Pork Roast with Apricot Glaze   266
Pork-Vegetable Stew   73
Pork with a Cranberry Glaze   269
Pot Roast and Veggies   146
Potato and Leek Soup   37
Potato Soup Plus!   28
Potatoes al Grande   121
Pretty Parsley Potatoes   120
Promising Pork Chops   259

Q

Quick-Fix Chicken   211

R

Ranch Pork Chops   253
Roast and Vegetable Stew   74
Roasted New Potatoes   122

Roasted Red Pepper Tenderloin   273
Russian Chicken   213

S

Saffron Rice and Chicken   224
St. Pat's Noodles   131
Santa Fe Stew   72
Sauce for Fancy Meatballs   162
Saucy Cabbage Soup   36
Saucy Ham Loaf   278
Sauerkraut and Bratwurst   291
Sausage and Beans   290
Sausage and Rice   246
Sausage-Hamburger Dip   16
Sausage-Pineapple Bits   21
Sausage-Pizza Soup   50
Savory Broccoli and Cauliflower   99
Savory Chicken Fettuccini   215
Savory Pork Chops   253
Savory Steak   135
Scrumptious Chicken Breasts   216
Seafood
   Cheddar Crab Casserole   292
   Crab Chowder   89
   Crab Dip   9
   Crab-Artichoke Spread   20
   Oyster Chowder   92
   Shrimp and Chicken Jambalaya   96
   Shrimp and Ham Jambalaya   94

   Shrimp and Sausage Jambalaya   95
   Tuna OK Bake   291
   Unbelievable Crab Dip   9
Serious Bean Stew   71
Show Time Pork Roast   267
Shredded Brisket for Sandwiches   157
Shrimp and Chicken Jambalaya   96
Shrimp and Ham Jambalaya   94
Shrimp and Sausage Jambalaya   95
***Side Dishes* – See Veggies & Side Dishes**
Sloppy Joes   177
Slow Cooker Cordon Bleu   203
Smoked Brisket   153
Smothered Chicken Breasts   217
Smothered Pork Chop Dinner   251
So-Good Chicken   213
Soup with a Zip   36
Soup's On!
   A Different Stew   69
   Beans and Barley Soup   64
   Beans 'n Sausage Soup   65
   Beef and Barley Soup   64
   Beef and Black Bean Soup   62
   Beef and Noodle Soup   63
   Beefy Rice Soup   61
   Black Bean Soup   53
   Black-Eyed Soup   61
   Cajun Bean Soup   60
   Cheddar Soup Plus   60
   Cheesy Potato Soup   58

Chicken and Barley Soup   56

Chicken and Rice Soup   56

Chicken Chowder   91

Chicken-Pasta Soup   57

Chicken Stew   69

Chicken Stew over Biscuits   80

Chicken-Tortellini Stew   66

Chili Soup   55

Chunky Chili   87

Comfort Stew   79

Confetti-Chicken Soup   54

Corn-Ham Chowder   93

Country Chicken Chowder   90

Crab Chowder   89

Cream of Zucchini Soup   52

Creamy Vegetable Soup   51

Delicious Broccoli-Cheese Soup   43

Easy Chili   86

Enchilada Soup   48

French Onion Soup   46

Ham and Cabbage Stew   77

Ham, Bean and Pasta Soup   45

Ham-Vegetable Chowder   88

Hamburger Soup   49

Hearty Meatball Stew   77

Hungarian Stew   76

Italian Bean Soup   44

Italian-Vegetable Stew   76

Meatball and Veggie Stew   75

Meatball Soup   42

Meatball Stew   75

Mexican-Meatball Soup   28

Minestrone Soup   66

Navy Bean Soup   41

Olé! For Stew   74

Oyster Chowder   92

Pancho Villa Stew   68

Pasta-Veggie Soup   40

Pinto Bean-Vegetable Soup   43

Pizza Soup   39

Pork and Hominy Soup   38

Pork-Vegetable Stew   73

Potato and Leek Soup   37

Potato Soup Plus!   28

Roast and Vegetable Stew   74

Santa Fe Stew   72

Saucy Cabbage Soup   36

Sausage-Pizza Soup   50

Serious Bean Stew   71

Shrimp and Chicken Jambalaya   96

Shrimp and Ham Jambalaya   94

Shrimp and Sausage Jambalaya   95

Soup with a Zip   36

South-of-the-Border Beef Stew   78

Southern Ham Stew   70

Southern Soup   35

Spicy Sausage Soup   33

Split-Pea and Ham Chowder   92

Taco-Chili Soup   32

Taco Soup   30

Taco Soup Olé   31

Tasty Black Bean Soup   49

Tasty Cabbage and Beef Soup   55

Tasty Chicken and Rice Soup   29

Tortellini Soup   47

Tortilla Soup   34

Traditional Chili   84

Turkey and Mushroom Soup   50

Turkey-Tortilla Soup   59

Turkey-Veggie Chili   85

Vegetable Chili   83

Vegetable-Lentil Soup   58

Vegetarian Chili   82

White Lightning Chili   81

Winter Minestrone   67

South-of-the-Border Beef Stew   78

Southern Chicken   234

Southern Ham Stew   70

Southern Soup   35

Southwest Spaghetti   162

Southwestern Chicken Pot   218

Special Ham Supper   283

Special Hot Dog Supper   178

Spicy Franks   24

Spicy Sausage Soup   33

Spicy Spanish Rice   129

Spicy Swiss Steak   137

Spinach-Stuffed Pork Roast   271

Split-Pea and Ham Chowder   92

Squash Combo   111

Stroganoff   138

Stuffed Cabbage   163

Stuffed Pork Chops   249

Stupendous Rice and Chicken   238

Sunday Chicken   219

Sunny Yellow Squash   112

Sunshine Green Beans   101

Super Corn   114

Surprise Dessert   300

Sweet-and-Hot Mustard   278

Sweet-and-Sour Beef   147

Sweet-and-Sour Chicken   218

Sweet-and-Sour Sausage Links   279

Sweet and Savory Brisket   154

Sweet and Spicy Chicken   233

Sweet Potatoes and Pineapple   127

Swiss Steak   135

T

Taco Chicken   228

Taco-Chili Soup   32

Taco Soup   30

Taco Soup Olé   31

Tangy Apricot Ribs   276

Tangy Chicken   221

Tangy Chicken Legs   228

Tasty Black Bean Soup   49

Tasty Cabbage and Beef Soup   55

Tasty Chicken and Rice Soup   29

Tasty Chicken and Veggies 223
Tasty Chicken-Rice and Veggies 220
Tender Pork Loin 270
Teriyaki Steak 139
Teriyaki Wingettes 22
Terrific Pork Tenderloin 270
The Best Ever Brisket 158
The Big Dipper 17
Three Hour Chicken 239
Tortellini Italian-Style 288
Tortellini Soup 47
Tortilla Soup 34
Traditional Chili 84
Tuna OK Bake 291
Turkey – **See Chicken & Turkey**
Turkey and Mushroom Soup 50
Turkey Bake 241
Turkey Cassoulet 244
Turkey Loaf 242
Turkey Spaghetti 243
Turkey-Tortilla Soup 59
Turkey-Veggie Chili 85

U

Unbelievable Crab Dip 9

V

Vegetable Chili 83
Vegetable-Lentil Soup 58

Vegetarian Chili 82
Veggies & Side Dishes
A Different Bean 106
Beans and More Beans 106
Better Butter Beans 107
Broccoli and Cheese 100
Broccoli-Cheese Bake 99
Cajun Beans and Rice 105
California Vegetables 119
Carnival Couscous 131
Cheese-Please Spinach 116
Cheese-Spaghetti and Spinach 132
Cheesy Ranch Potatoes 128
Cheezy Potatoes 126
Chili Frijoles 109
Cinnamon Carrots 110
Company Broccoli 101
Company Potatoes 126
Creamed Cheese Spinach 115
Creamed New Potatoes 120
Creamed Peas and Potatoes 115
Creamy Limas 108
Crunchy Couscous 130
Crunchy Green Beans 105
Delicious Risotto Rice 130
Dressed-Up Hash Browns 125
Easy Baked Potatoes 124
Four Veggie Bake 118
Glazed Sweet Potatoes 128
Glory Potatoes 124

Golden Squash 113

Golden Veggies 118

Good Old Cheesy Potatoes 123

Green Bean Revenge 104

Green Beans to Enjoy 103

Harvest-Vegetable Casserole 117

Healthy Veggies 117

Hoppin' John 129

Italian Beans 107

Krazy Karrots 111

Potatoes al Grande 121

Pretty Parsley Potatoes 120

Roasted New Potatoes 122

St. Pat's Noodles 131

Savory Broccoli and Cauliflower 99

Spicy Spanish Rice 129

Squash Combo 111

Sunny Yellow Squash 112

Sunshine Green Beans 101

Super Corn 114

Sweet Potatoes and Pineapple 127

Yummy Corn 114

W

Walnut Ham 279

Western Pork Supper 255

White Lightning Chili 81

Whiz Bang Dip 17

Wingettes in Honey Sauce 23

Winter Dinner 214

Winter Minestrone 67

Y

Yes to This Chicken 240

Yummy Corn 114

Z

Zesty Ham Supper 280

Cookbooks Published by
Cookbook Resources, LLC
Bringing Family and Friends to the Table

*The Best of Cooking
with 3 Ingredients*

*The Ultimate Cooking
with 4 Ingredients*

*Easy Cooking
with 5 Ingredients*

*Healthy Cooking
with 4 Ingredients*

*Gourmet Cooking
with 5 Ingredients*

*4-Ingredient Recipes
for 30-Minute Meals*

*Essential 3-4-5
Ingredient Recipes*

The Best 1001 Short, Easy Recipes

1001 Fast Easy Recipes

1001 Community Recipes

*Busy Woman's
Quick & Easy Recipes*

*Busy Woman's
Slow Cooker Recipes*

Easy Slow Cooker Cookbook

Easy One-Dish Meals

Easy Potluck Recipes

Easy Casseroles

Easy Desserts

Sunday Night Suppers

Easy Church Suppers

365 Easy Meals

365 Easy Chicken Recipes

365 Easy Soups and Stews

365 Easy Vegetarian Recipes

Quick Fixes with Cake Mixes

*Kitchen Keepsakes/
More Kitchen Keepsakes*

Gifts for the Cookie Jar

*All New Gifts
for the Cookie Jar*

Muffins In A Jar

The Big Bake Sale Cookbook

*Classic Tex-Mex
and Texas Cooking*

Classic Southwest Cooking

Miss Sadie's Southern Cooking

Texas Longhorn Cookbook

Cookbook 25 Years

A Little Taste of Texas

A Little Taste of Texas II

*Trophy Hunters'
Wild Game Cookbook*

Recipe Keeper

*Leaving Home Cookbook
and Survival Guide*

*Classic Pennsylvania
Dutch Cooking*

Easy Diabetic Recipes

cookbook resources® LLC

www.cookbookresources.com

Your Ultimate Source for Easy Cookbooks

365 Easy
Slow Cooker
Recipes

cookbook
resources® LLC

www.cookbookresources.com